A COMPREHENSIVE GUIDE TO

Indian Scriptures

SUNITA PANT BANSAL

Readomania

Readomania
An imprint of Kurious Kind Media Private Limited
readomania.com
email: contact@readomania.com
Facebook: facebook.com/iamreadomania
Twitter: twitter.com/iamreadomania
Instagram: iamreadomania

First Published in 2024 by Readomania

Edited by Indrani Ganguly (Managing Editor, Readomania)

ISBN: 978-81-978775-7-5

Typeset in Palatino Linotype by Shine Graphics
Printed in Delhi

CONTENTS

AUTHOR'S NOTE

The captivating world of Hindu scriptures and mythology was introduced to me by my paternal grandparents during my early years in primary school. The journey began with stories of gods and goddesses who inhabited my grandmother's puja room. Gradually, these stories expanded to include the trees, flowers, rivers, and mountains, eventually encompassing even the sun, moon, and the solar system. As I grew older and began to read, I found myself drawn to my grandfather's library, which housed scriptures, philosophical commentaries, and biographies of saints and spiritual masters.

Although my grandparents are no longer with me, the treasure trove they left behind continues to reveal its gems, one after another.

I am immensely grateful to my publisher, Dipankar Mukherjee, for encouraging me to write this guidebook. Revisiting my decades of research and notes, I have had the opportunity to dive deep into the vast ocean of Hindu scriptures, distil their essence, and organise them systematically to create a fair and impartial reference guide for readers of any faith.

For over three decades, I have written books on Hindu mythology for readers of all ages. Popular mythology often focuses on the battles between gods and demons, with good triumphing over evil, or the life stories of key figures from the *Ramayana* and the *Mahabharata*. While I have explored these themes in my work, my aim with this guidebook is different.

Few people venture beyond the surface to explore the metaphors hidden within these ancient texts. Those who wish to, often find themselves wondering: How many Hindu scriptures are there? Which is the oldest? Which is the most important? What order should they be read in? How long are they, and will I be able to understand them? This guidebook is designed to answer those very questions.

Unlike many existing books that rely on commentaries from well-known scholars, I have consciously chosen not to include interpretations. The scriptures are presented here as they are, free from the lens of history, politics, or social contexts. I believe it is essential for readers to engage with the texts themselves and form their own interpretations. My hope is to offer a glimpse into our rich scriptural heritage and inspire curiosity for deeper exploration.

Condensing the vast array of scriptures into a concise format was no small feat.

The development of Hinduism can be compared to the growth of a banyan tree. This unique tree sends roots downward, which eventually become trunks in their own right, making it difficult to discern the original trunk amidst the sprawling branches. Similarly, Hinduism has evolved over millennia, giving rise to numerous belief systems, while the older ones still thrive. With no single founder, no central authority, no definitive scripture, and no fixed doctrine, Hinduism eludes traditional classification, making confusion an understandable part of the exploration.

Another challenge in writing this guidebook was assigning dates to the scriptures. Many of these texts were originally passed down orally and only later committed to writing, making it difficult to pinpoint their origins. Scholarly debate over their timelines further complicates this task, so I have refrained from delving into date disputes.

What is clear is that the Vedas are the oldest of Hindu scriptures, with the Upanishads forming the latter portion. All texts following the Vedas are categorised as Smriti. The bulk of Hindu scriptures were composed before the advent of Christianity.

The chapters of this guidebook largely follow the historical development of these scriptures. The Vedas—including the Samhitas, Brahmanas, Aranyakas, and Upanishads—are the most ancient and revered, so they form the starting point. Each of the 108 Upanishads is linked to a specific Veda and is discussed in its respective chapter. Together, these texts comprise what is known as Shruti—the primary philosophical texts, believed to contain all knowledge of the universe.

Subsequent scriptures fall under the category of Smriti, which are practical applications of the philosophical teachings found in the Shruti. This includes texts such as the Dharma Shastras, Puranas, Itihasas, Vedangas, Upa Vedas, Darshanas, Vedanta Sutras, Agamas, and Kala Shastras.

Rituals and festivals are important in Hinduism, but this guidebook does not delve into them. I believe rituals are deeply personal choices, and while they may differ from person to person, they often seek similar goals. Hinduism's flexibility allows individuals within the same family to have their own chosen deities.

India, with its vast cultural diversity, reflects this same flexibility. The subcontinent's rich variety of languages, regional identities, sects, and social statuses has created an overwhelming tapestry of beliefs and practices. For Hindus, diversity is integral to life, which is why one person's practice may differ greatly from another's. While this has left Hinduism without a centralised doctrine, it has also made the tradition incredibly resilient and adaptable.

Hinduism is not just a religion; it is a way of life. Correct behaviour is emphasised across daily activities, and not limited to specific rituals or practices. I recognise that some readers may skim through this guidebook, but I hope that many will pause when they encounter something that piques their curiosity—be it the existence of multiple Gitas or *Ramayanas* or references to 'scientific advances' in the Vedas. When that moment of interest occurs, this guidebook will have served its purpose.

Sunita Pant Bansal
New Delhi, 2024

INTRODUCTION

Hinduism differs from all the other religions of the world, as it has no single founder, system or God, and neither does it have a single belief of mode of worship. As a religion, it is highly democratic. One can follow any path prescribed by the scriptures, any God of one's choice suiting one's temperament.

The Hindu religion is called Sanatana Dharma, where *sanatana* stands for eternal and *dharma* for laws. So, Sanatana Dharma means the eternal, imperishable cosmic laws or the laws of nature. This makes Hinduism a way of life lived in accordance with the cosmic laws.

Unlike other religions that have few books, Hinduism has hundreds of voluminous scriptures written in Sanskrit, spanning millennia. *A Comprehensive Guide to Indian Scriptures* is written for those who have an interest in knowing about Hinduism but do not know where and how to start. This book is meant to guide them by categorising the bewildering range of Hindu scriptures, and presenting their essence in a simple manner.

The Hindu scriptures are divided into two broad categories—Shruti and Smriti.

Shruti consists of the Vedas. All the other scriptures that have the Vedas as their basis fall under Smriti. Vedas are written in Vedic Sanskrit and the Smriti scriptures in classical Sanskrit that was spoken by the people of that time.

Shruti means what is heard. The sages did not create the Vedas. They heard the eternal truths that God revealed to them.

Hence the Vedas are superhuman texts, the earliest knowledge of mankind, the most valuable treasure, the oldest scriptures on earth. The Vedas are the roots of Hindu culture and wisdom... and it is believed that they are the source of all other scriptures of the world as well. There are four Vedas—Rig, Yajur, Sama, and Atharva. They follow two basic themes, truth and eternal order, the ultimate goal being the well-being of all living creatures, their spiritual upliftment and liberation.

Smriti are the secondary scriptures based on the teachings of the Vedas. They are the recollections of the experiences of the ancient seers. The Smriti scriptures comprise Purana, Itihasa, Vedanga, Upa Veda, Darshana, Vedanta Sutra, Agama, Kala Shastra, and also other writings based on the Vedas. The Smriti are also collectively known as the Dharma Shastra, as they lay down the laws for regulating the individual, family, social and national obligations of people. They explain the codes of conduct for mankind in day-to-day life.

This book presents a brief overview of the Veda, Dharma Shastra, Purana, the great epics *Ramayana* and *Mahabharata*, Bhagavad Gita, Vedanga, Upa Veda, Darshana, Vedanta Sutra, Agama, Kala Shastra, and other important texts. Such an overview of literature that spans millennia cannot be comprehensive. It has to be selective. Hence, only the essential ideas are presented.

It is tough to assign precise dates to the Hindu scriptures. Most of the texts were orally created, recited, transmitted, and were put down in written form much later, making it difficult to date them accurately. However, what is known with certainty is that the Vedas are the most ancient scriptures, dated approximately 1800–800 BCE. They were followed by the Upanishads, from 700 BCE up to 1500 CE, including the minor Upanishads. Meanwhile, the Darshana, Brahma Sutra,

Ramayana, Mahabharata were created in 500–200 BCE, followed by the Smriti texts in 100 BCE–300 CE. The Purana evolved over centuries from 400 BCE to 1000 CE.

A Comprehensive Guide to Indian Scriptures serves to showcase the essence of Hinduism and provide a basis for further study.

1
SHRUTI OR VEDA

The Vedas are accorded the highest position in the Hindu scriptures. The Hindu religion is also referred to as Vedic religion, because all later texts, including the Bhagavad Gita accept the supremacy of the Vedas.

Veda comes from the Sanskrit root *vid*, meaning 'to know', hence the term *veda* signifies knowledge. The Vedas were revealed by God through sacred sounds to ancient sages, heard by them during intense meditation. These sages transmitted them to their disciples. The Vedas say that they are the breath of God—God and the Vedas are as closely connected as we are to our breath.

There is nothing in the Vedas themselves to indicate when they were composed. It is believed that they were mostly composed sometime between 1800–800 BCE. There are varied opinions regarding the antiquity of the Vedas, but all conclude that they existed even before the formation of the universe. The spiritual interpretation is that the Divine Truth always existed and was revealed to the sages in their higher states of consciousness. It is similar to the scientific view that knowledge has always existed, the scientists merely discover that knowledge, for example, gravity existed before Newton discovered it.

Understanding the Vedic truths is more important than trying to fix the date of their origin, since the latter can never be ascertained with precision. Of all the scriptures in the world, the Vedas alone are liberal in philosophy, saying that knowing or learning them is not essential. The Vedas do not insist that there is only one way of leading a good life. They say that any path followed with sincerity will lead to the same goal.

The Vedas predate idol worship. They refer to *devas*, meaning the bright ones, who are the manifestations of different aspects of the One, Supreme God. Vedic devas or deities include Agni, Indra, Ashvins, Maruts, Ribhus, Rudra, Vayu, Brihaspati, Vishnu, Usha, Saraswati, and Mitra-Varuna. Worship done through the prescribed rituals invokes these devas. But then, there is no idol worship, and there are no temples dedicated to Vedic devas.

The ancient sages first composed the hymns of the Rig Veda offering them to God, the Great Spirit. *Rig* means verse and *veda* means spiritual knowledge of how all things in the universe came into existence and for what purpose. This was the first Hindu scripture.

Subsequently, the brahmins or the priests made anthologies from the Rig Veda, which were put together to make the Yajur Veda, a manual for the brahmins to conduct sacrifices. Another collection from Rig Veda was made, called the Sama Veda, a collection of hymns for chanting while making offerings to God. A fourth collection called Atharva Veda was made much later. It contained common healing practices, superstitions and folklore.

Initially, the knowledge of Vedas was imparted orally to successive generations. This process continued for many centuries before they were written down. It was Sage Vyasa who compiled and classified them about 5,000 years ago and wrote them down on the banks of river Saraswati. After arranging them in their present form, he distributed them to his four disciples. The sage gave Rig Veda to Paila, Sama Veda to Jaimini, Yajur Veda to Vaishampayana, and Atharva Veda to Sumantu. These four sages taught them to their disciples, who passed them to the later generations and so on.

Science talks about the world being embraced by the concepts of time and space. The Vedas advocate that truth can be realised only by freeing oneself from the concepts of time and space. This is possible only when we turn our gaze inwards, in which we forget ourselves as in deep sleep. The common goal of the Vedas is the well-being of living creatures, the upliftment of individual Self or *jeevatma* and finally, the union of *jeevatma* with *paramatma* or God. In essence, the Vedas aim at liberation of Self while living in the world.

Each Veda has four sections, the first one is the Samhita containing prayers and invocations to Vedic deities. The second one is the Brahmana that explains the meaning of prayers and gives instructions for rituals. The third is Aranyaka, giving symbolic and philosophical meanings of the prayers. The last section is the Vedanta or Upanishad, doing away completely with rituals and gods, and exploring the nature Ultimate Reality and how we can reach the goal of life.

But then, the four divisions of the vast ancient Indian Vedic literature are not fixed but fluid. There is no absolute universally true distinction between Aranyakas and Brahmanas. Likewise, there is no absolute distinction between Aranyakas and Upanishads, as some Upanishads are incorporated in a few Aranyakas.

As a student, a *brahmachari*, one is advised to chant mantras and lead a controlled and virtuous life, following the Samhitas. As a householder or *grihastha*, one is expected to observe the injunctions of the Brahmanas. In the third stage of life, namely *vanaprastha*, which is the forest dweller's stage, one is supposed to meditate upon the underlying spiritual truths behind the rituals, as found in Aranyakas and practise renunciation. Finally, as stated in the Upanishads, as a *sannyasi*, one has to seek the ultimate truth and know Brahman for liberating oneself.

Other than yoga, meditation, self-realisation and such spiritual subjects, the Vedas also talk about all the sciences as we know them today.

While the Greeks spoke of a flat earth, the Vedas had long ago declared that earth was round, and it revolved around the sun which was the centre of the solar system. And that the solar system was held together by the gravitational pull of the sun and the planets. It was many centuries later that Newton discovered gravity.

Vedic literature shows that ancient Indians knew about atoms and quantum physics. The complete atomic structure is explained in the Rig Veda. All elements have the same source of energy that the Vedic sages called Chaitanya, which though invisible, can be perceived through several of its manifestations. Modern scientists agree and state that the invisible energy is seen through objects like the electrical energy is seen through lighted bulbs.

According to the Vedas, Prakriti is the building block of universe. Before the creation of universe, an amazing property of Prakriti, its dual behaviour, is described in the Rig Veda. Individually, it behaves like a particle and collectively, it behaves like energy. This period is called Pralaya Kaal, meaning a period of no-creation (or total disintegration). The only thing existing in this period is a mysterious mist, a group of particles, densely filling everywhere like an ocean of stagnant energy. No life exists as nothing is created, nor does death exist as there is nothing to die. During Pralaya Kaal, everything is inert and inactive. On arrival of the creation period, the substance of the stagnant energy becomes active and turns into the raw material for the creation of the universe. Clearly, the material cause of the creation of everything is this energy, which according to the Vedas was in the form of particles. This resonates with the particle physics theories of today.

In the Vedas, Kalpa describes the cyclical process of the beginning and the end of the universe. This is in conformity with the findings of modern physics. The term light years for measuring time was known to ancient Indians as Kalpa, which is the period between the beginning and the end of the universe.

Atharva Veda has detailed descriptions of human and animal anatomy, including the skeletal, muscular, circulatory, nervous and digestive systems. It also has the science of healing, called Ayurveda, or the ancient Indian indigenous medical science.

Astronomy, astrology, mathematics, architecture, wireless communication, science of making aircraft and weapons. including atomic bomb, were all part of Vedic literature.

2

SAMHITA, BRAHMANA, ARANYAKA

SAMHITA

The Vedic Samhitas are methodical collections of sacred sounds or mantras, prayers, hymns, litanies and benedictions petitioning nature or Vedic deities.

A Samhita is the first portion of a Veda, a collection of sacred mantras having divine powers. The inspired seer or the author of the mantra is known as a *rishi* and the object with which it is concerned is called a *devta*. A *devta* may not necessarily be a deity or God, it could be a weapon, or any other inanimate object being invoked for a specific purpose.

Mantras are chanted to propitiate the celestial gods during yajnas (fire-sacrifice), to protect oneself from evil forces, and for seeking assistance in performing one's duties in life. There are more than 20,000 mantras, addressing the mystery of creation, divinity, aspects of nature, everyday life and behaviour. The effectiveness of the mantras depends on the mental discipline, correct breathing, and recitation. They are to be chanted in the tune prescribed in the Vedas.

The Rig Veda Samhita has 1,028 hymns in about 10,600 mantras. Arranged in 21 sections, the Yajur Veda has 1,875 mantras, the Sama Veda also has 1,875 mantras and the Atharva Veda has 6,000 mantras. In all, the Veda Samhitas have a little more than 20,000 distinct mantras in ancient Sanskrit.

Given the large number of mantras, there are bound to be differences in interpretations. It is believed that whatever meaning appeals to a sincere student is the right meaning for that person, as it resonates with their inner nature, helping them in their religious or spiritual life.

Some well-known books written in the post-Vedic period are also called Samhitas because the word *samhita* means systematic compilation of knowledge. Vedic Samhitas are not to be confused with them. Some of the popular post-Vedic Samhitas are Bhrigu Samhita, Charaka Samhita, Sushruta Samhita, etc.

BRAHMANA

The brahmins produced a literature of their own, interpreting and explaining the Vedic rituals, ceremonies and sacrifices. This literature is called the Brahmanas, constituting the second portion of a Veda. They explain the mantras of the Samhitas, and Vedic sacrifices, as well as how they are to be performed.

Basically, the Brahmanas are guides for the proper performance of rituals and sacrifices, explaining the rules and regulations in great details. They also outline the performance of various religious duties and discuss the rituals that are performed for specific purpose with the objective of getting a specific effect. How a mantra is to be used by the householder while performing the rituals, which yajna is to be performed in what manner, description of the worship of various forms of God, description of the offerings, the origin and meaning of the yajnas, are elaborately explained. The fire-God Agni, to whom all the offerings are made during the yajnas, has an important place in the Brahmanas.

The ancients claimed that all that one wishes to have can be obtained by performing the Vedic rituals in proper manner, with the knowledge of their real meaning but not with their mechanical performance. The rituals are so powerful that they can even make the performer control the process of nature.

Apart from explaining the symbolism and meaning of the Samhita, the Brahmanas also expound scientific knowledge including astronomy and geometry.

It is believed that the number of Brahmanas that existed in ancient times was around 1,180. Unfortunately, most were lost to the ravages of time, invasions and atrocities of the foreign rulers.

ARANYAKA

After Brahmanas came the Aranyakas, meaning belonging to the forest, written by holy men who left the material world to contemplate on life's problems in the spiritual thought world. They give mystical, symbolic and philosophical interpretations in metaphysical terms and deeper meanings of the mantras of Samhitas and rituals of Brahmanas, giving the logical reasoning behind following them.

Aranyakas are intended for those who are in the third stage of life, which is *vanaprastha*, preparing them for the fourth stage, *sannyasa*. The emphasis is more on knowledge and meditation rather than chanting mantras or performing rituals. Out of the 1,180 Aranyakas, only a few are available now.

These truths, the fruit of meditation in the forests, were the source of the Upanishads, the most important Hindu scriptures after the Rig Veda.

The Aranyakas along with the Brahmanas represent the emerging transitions in later Vedic religious practices. The transition culminates with the blossoming of ancient Indian philosophy from external sacrificial rituals to internalised philosophical treatise of the Upanishads.

The Aranyakas constitute the Upasana Kanda, concerned with different kinds of worship and meditation, and form 19 percent of the Vedas. The Upanishads constitute the Gyana Kanda, or the knowledge section talking about the highest knowledge of Nirguna Brahman and showing the path of God realisation, forming 6 percent of the Vedas.

The Aranyakas and the Upanishads impart spiritual knowledge leading to liberation, or freedom from ignorance and sorrows of life, and the realisation of the ultimate truth.

3

RIG VEDA AND SAMA VEDA

RIG VEDA

The Rig Veda is the oldest and the most magnificent of all Vedas. It's the most ancient text in Sanskrit, the oldest religious scripture in the world, and the oldest collection of ideas known to mankind. The other three Vedas are based on the Rig Veda.

The Rig Veda has four layers—Samhita, Brahmanas, Aranyakas and Upanishads.

Rig Veda Samhita is a collection of 1,028 hymns divided into 10 *mandalas* or sections, written by different sages and their clans.

The hymns are primarily dedicated to praising the Rigvedic deities or nature gods. Then there are also hymns dealing with the philosophical speculations about the origin of the universe and the nature of mankind. The third group of hymns are those dealing with social, political and secular subjects. There are prayers for various favours like health, long life, progeny, victory in war, destruction of enemies, glory, protection and guidance. The Veda also contains hymns related to astrology, astronomy, ayurveda, yoga, meditation, as well use of various kinds of weapons, horses and chariots in warfare.

The gods mentioned in the Rig Veda are those associated with heaven, air and earth.

Indra is the chief god mentioned in the Rig Veda. Regarded as the most powerful, he is the Lord of heaven, war, and thunder. His mount is a white elephant called Airavata and his weapon is called Vajra (thunderbolt), made for him by Tvastar, the builder of divine weapons. Vasus are the attendants of Indra. They are Dhara the earth, Anala the fire, Apa the water, Anila the wind, Dhruva the pole star, Soma the moon, and Prabhasa the light.

Agni, the fire-God, occupies an equally important place as Indra, as he is considered a link between God and us. He is the Lord of sacrifices and a messenger carrying our offerings to gods.

Vishnu is the Lord of all the three worlds. He is a minor god in the Rig Veda and is one of the Adityas. The Adityas are solar deities. They personify the universal law and are 12 in number, described as the 12 spokes of a wheel that corresponds to the 12 months in a year. They are Mitra, Varuna, Aryaman, Daksha, Bhaga, Amsa, Tvastar, Savitar, Pushan, Sakra, Vivasvat, and Vishnu. They uphold the law of nature, illumine the world, drive away darkness, and nourish all living beings.

Varuna is the chief of Adityas and the compassionate ruler of the earth and heaven. He is the Lord of the oceans, night sky, and rain. He is considered as the Lord enforcing natural order. He is the upholder of moral law, providing justice to all. He punishes those who deviate from the natural law and commit sin, but pardons them when they repent for their misdeeds. He is considered as the knower and controller of one and all.

Savitar, one of the Adityas, is the Sun of very early morning hidden by dark night. He upholds law, drives away sickness, and pardons our sins. The famous Gayatri mantra is addressed to Savitar for enlightenment.

Surya is the chief of solar deities. He is extremely brilliant and bright. He is the giver of power, strength, health, and brilliance. Saranya is the goddess of clouds, the daughter of Tvastar, and the wife of Surya.

Usha is the daughter of the sky, and the goddess of early morning who brings hope, happiness, riches, light, beauty, and all good things in life.

Vayu is the vital breath, and the Lord of thought. He is invisible, intelligent, and is swift as wind. He is the protector, Lord of medicines, and is the one who illumines the earth and heaven.

The two Ashvins are the twin horsemen and sons of Saranya, the Goddess of clouds. They are the brothers of Usha, the dawn. They symbolise sunrise and sunset. Regarded as the deities of Ayurvedic medicines, they have healing and curative powers. The Ashvins are supposed to descend on the earth thrice a day to cure diseases of people.

Prithvi is the Goddess of earth, and Dyaus, the God of the sky and husband of Prithvi. Pushan is a pastoral God. He is the Lord of all paths, prosperity, marriages, journeys, roads, guardian of cattle, who drives away enemies, and is responsible for inducing thoughts. He also protects people from wild animals and helps them to tread on the path without any difficulty.

The Rig Veda has three Brahmanas: Aitareya, Shankhayana and Kaushitaki.

Aitareya Brahmana, also known as Ashvalayana Brahmana, has eight Panchikas or books of five chapters each. Altogether there are 40 chapters. Aitareya Brahmana deals mainly with the Soma sacrifice, worship and royal ceremonies, explaining about the various sacrifices performed by the kshatriyas and the mutual relationship between brahmins and kshatriyas. It is believed that Sage Mahidasa Aitareya composed the first 30 chapters and Sage Shaunaka added the last 10 chapters to it later.

The Aitareya Brahmana states, "The sun never really sets or rises. In that they think of him 'He is setting,' having reached the end of the day, he inverts himself; thus he makes evening below, day above. Again in that they think of him 'He is rising in the morning,' having reached the end of the night he inverts himself; thus he makes day below, night above. He never sets; indeed he never sets."

Shankhayana Brahmana mainly deals with sacrifices or yajnas. It has 30 chapters. Its content is similar to that of the Aitareya Brahmana, but more logical and scientific, and arranged in a more systematic manner.

Kaushitaki Brahmana differs from Shankhayana in a few words and syllables at some places. In this Brahmana, the sentences are also enumerated. It also deals with sacrifices or yajnas. It is believed that these two Brahmanas once existed as a single text, which was eventually divided into two.

The Rig Veda has three Aranyakas: Aitareya, Shankhayana and Taittiriya.

Aitareya Aranyaka talks about the ceremony Mahavrata or the great vow of fundamental duties, giving ritualistic as well as mystical explanations. It also teaches Prana Vidya, according to which, the vital breath that forms the life-breath is the same for all living beings. Shankhayana Aranyaka is similar to Aitareya Aranyaka but also teaches rituals that are antidotes for warding off death and sickness. It also explains the meaning and effect of dreams. Taittiriya Aranyaka teaches Surya namaskar, apart from being a treatise on yajnas.

There are 10 Upanishads associated with the Rig Veda.

Aitareya Upanishad is considered as one of the earliest Upanishads. It is associated with Sage Aitareya and is a part of Aitareya Aranyaka. It consists of 3 chapters with 33 verses. The earlier parts discuss the sacrificial ceremonies like Mahavrata and its interpretations. It gives a deeper meaning of the sacrifices with the aim to elevate the mind of man from outer ceremonial acts of worship through external sacrifices to the inner or inward sacrifice.

The Aitareya Upanishad also teaches about creation. In the beginning there was only the Absolute Self and nothing else. He, out of his own will, created the entire universe. To guard the universe, he created the various deities and man. Then, he created the sense organs, from which powers and aspects emerged. Speech emerged from mouth, breath from nostrils, and so on.

The eight directions emerged from death. He created divine beings, who were given different duties to perform. The Self asked them to enter the respective parts of man. Fire entered the mouth as speech, sun entered the eyes as rays of sight, and so on. In this manner, the various divinities entered man and man became divine.

This Upanishad is also known for its philosophy of Atman or consciousness as the intellect. According to it, intelligence is Brahman, and all living creatures and the five elements namely earth, wind, space, water and fire are the creation of that intelligence. Everything in the universe is guided by and is also based on this consciousness that is Brahman.

Akshamalika Upanishad is dedicated to the use and significance of *akshamala* (prayer beads) in spiritual practices. It explains the symbolic meaning of the beads and their association with various deities, highlighting their role in meditation and mantra recitation. The text states that the *akshamala* represents divine consciousness, and regular use helps in purifying the mind and focusing on one's spiritual goals. It stresses that by chanting sacred mantras with devotion using the beads, one can achieve self-realisation and liberation.

Atmabodha Upanishad explains at length about the sacred mantra, AUM that is considered as the innermost Brahman and about Lord Narayana who exists in all. It says that Brahman exists as knowledge in the middle of the heart and the knowledge of Aham Brahmasmi (I am Brahman) goes beyond Maya.

Bahvricha Upanishad is about the Supreme Power, the Goddess who alone existed in the beginning of creation. From her being, Brahman was born and later everything else was born. She is the consciousness within and is the Maha Tripura Sundari. She is Atman, she is Brahman, she is consciousness, and everything that assumes various forms.

Kaushitaki Upanishad explores the nature of the soul (atman), life after death, and the concept of rebirth. It discusses the journey of the soul after death and the importance of understanding Brahman, the Ultimate Reality. The Upanishad emphasises that through knowledge and realisation of Brahman, one can transcend the cycle of birth and death. It also touches on the nature of consciousness and its connection with the divine, offering insights into the metaphysical and spiritual dimensions of existence. This Upanishad considers the vital breath or Prana as the prime mover or Brahman.

Mudgala Upanishad elaborates on the cosmic significance of the Purusha Sukta, a hymn that describes the cosmic being, Purusha, as the source of all creation. The Upanishad emphasises the role of Purusha as the all-encompassing divine entity, whose sacrifice led to the creation of the universe and all beings. It further explores how the different parts of Purusha correspond to various aspects of the cosmos, showcasing the unity of existence. The text highlights the importance of realising Purusha as the Ultimate Reality for spiritual liberation.

Nadabindu Upanishad focuses on the concept of Nada (sound) as a path to spiritual realisation. It emphasises the practice of Nada Yoga, where meditative focus on internal sound leads to higher states of consciousness and ultimately to union with Brahman, the Supreme Reality. The text explains that the 'sound' begins as a hum and gradually refines into the sacred syllable AUM, symbolising the underlying vibration of the universe. By meditating on this internal sound, one can transcend worldly distractions, calm the mind, and attain spiritual liberation.

Nirvana Upanishad teaches that knowledge results in the burning up of the notion of existence or non-existence of causal, subtle, gross bodies and egoistic feelings. Then one becomes the very Brahman, the eternal form.

Saubhagyalakshmi Upanishad imparts knowledge through Lakshmi, the Goddess of prosperity. It discusses Maya, the dissolution of mind, concentration, and the attainment of bliss. The text also explains yogic practices through tantric concepts of the nine chakras: the basic Brahmachakra of root, followed by Svadhishthana (sacral), Nabhi (navel), Anahata (heart), Kantha (throat), Talu (palate), Ajna (brow), Nirvana, and finally the Akashi chakra of Space.

Tripura Upanishad is dedicated to the worship of the Goddess Tripura, representing the three states of consciousness: waking, dreaming, and deep sleep. It emphasises on Shakti, the divine feminine power, and describes the worship of Tripura Sundari, highlighting the unity of the individual soul with cosmic consciousness.

GAYATRI MANTRA

The Gayatri Mantra of the Rig Veda is one of the most revered and powerful mantras in Hinduism. It is a prayer dedicated to Savitar, the Sun-god, and is recited for enlightenment, wisdom, and spiritual awakening.

The mantra is as follows:

Om bhur bhuvah svah, tatsavitur varenyam, bhargo devasya dhimahi, dhiyo yo nah prachodayat.

This mantra seeks to meditate on the divine light of the Creator, asking for enlightenment and guidance of the intellect toward righteousness and wisdom. The mantra is not only a prayer for wisdom but also a meditation on the universal energy that sustains life. It is believed to purify the mind, enhance spiritual growth, and lead to self-realisation. Reciting the mantra is thought to align the individual with the cosmic forces, promoting inner peace and clarity.

SAMA VEDA

Sama Veda is the book of songs, the wisdom of chants, and the origin of Indian music. It is the Veda of hymns representing the ecstasy of spiritual knowledge and the power of devotion. Many of the Rig Vedic hymns are set to music in Sama Veda. In Bhagavad Gita, Lord Krishna says, "Among the Vedas, I am Sama Veda." *Sama* means 'that which brings peace'.

It is believed that originally there were many rituals that became intricate and elaborate as time passed on. Thus emerged the need for compilation of all the rituals and chants in a separate book, as a guide to the priests who sung them. This compilation eventually became the Sama Veda.

The Sama Veda Samhita is not meant to be read like a text, it has to be heard. The text, like a musical score sheet, contains notated melodies, probably the world's oldest surviving ones. The musical notations are written usually immediately above, sometimes within, the lines of the text, either in syllabic or numerical form. Out of the 1,875 verses in this Veda, 1,800 are from the Rig Veda.

Sama Veda Samhita is in two parts. The first part is the melody collection called Purvarchaka or the first adoration of the deities and the second part is Uttararchaka or the later adoration through rituals.

Just like the Rig Veda, the Sama Veda begins with Agni and Indra hymns but shifts to abstract speculations and philosophy. The prayers are for guidance, for destroying darkness by giving light, for blessing one with wealth and happiness, and to protect one by destroying one's enemies. The Veda clearly explains how the hymns must be sung by giving emphasis to the sounds of the mantras that have effect on the environment and the person who sings them.

The Sama Veda stresses the importance of mild speech, cleanliness, fulfilling one's vows, performing good deeds, perseverance, charity, and imparting knowledge to others. It also mentions the importance of control over senses, yoga, hard work, good actions, speaking the truth, keeping good company, engaging oneself in pious and religious activities, noble deeds and meditation.

There are 10 Brahmanas in the Sama Veda. Out of these, the main or the important ones are Tandya, Shadavimsha and Jaiminiya Brahmanas.

Tandya Brahmana or Praudha or 'great' Brahmana is also known as Panchavimsha Brahmana and Adbhut Brahmana, since it contains many miraculous stories. This Brahmana deals with general information about yajnas and the duties of the priests and has 25 sections. Shadavimsha Brahmana is the twenty-sixth section of the Panchavimsha Brahmana, quite like the appendix of a book. Jaiminiya Brahmana is fairly long and contains several Vedic legends and stories. In the last section of this Brahmana, geographical and historical information is given in details.

Samavidhana Brahmana of Sama Veda deals primarily with black magic. Devatadhyaya Brahmana details the Vedic metres. Vamsha Brahmana is a short Brahmana containing a list of ancient Sama Vedic teachers. The others are Arsheya, Chandogyopanishad, Jaiminiya Arsheya and Samhitopanishad Brahmanas.

Only Jaiminiya Aranyaka of the Sama Veda seems to be available.

The Sama Veda has 16 Upanishads. Two of them, Chandogya and Kena, are Mukhya or principal Upanishads. The others are Vajrasuchi, Maha, Savitri, Aruneya, Maitreya, Kundika, Brihat-Sannyasa, Vasudeva, Avyakta, Rudraksha, Maitrayani, Jabali, Yoga Chudamani and Darshana Upanishads. Together, they offer a unique gateway to understanding the transformative power of music and meditation within the spiritual journey.

Chandogya Upanishad is one of the oldest and longest of all Upanishads. It says that the one who is not conscious of his body, will not be affected either by desire or anger. A number of truths are explained in this Upanishad in the form of stories.

The initial chapters explain the rituals involved in Vedic sacrifices. The later chapters are concerned with the origin, profundity, and the importance of chanting the sacred mantra

AUM and how it is associated with the life breath or Prana. The doctrine of reincarnation is also stated as an ethical consequence of one's good or bad karma or actions. This Upanishad stresses the importance of sacrifice, austerity, charity, and the study of the Vedas under the guidance of a Guru. Further, it explains the value of speech, thought, meditation, understanding, strength, memory and hope.

A well-known story in this Upanishad is the dialogue between Satyakama Jabala and his mother. It asserts that the status of a brahmin comes from character, not by birth. For the one who realises the soul that is free of evil, age, death, sorrow and thirst, there is freedom in all the worlds.

Kena Upanishad is one of the primary Upanishads. Kena means 'by whom' or 'from what cause'. The Upanishad is divided into four sections, first two are poems and the last two are prose. The verses deal with the Absolute principle, the Supreme Brahman, that is behind the world of phenomenon and the prose deals with the Supreme as Ishvara or God.

In this Upanishad, Goddess Ambika or Uma appears as Jnanambika or the Goddess of Jnana or Supreme knowledge. She gives instructions about the doctrine of Brahman, knowledge or Supreme Reality to Indra, the King of the devas, when the devas in their arrogance fail to recognise the Supreme Being. The devas, after defeating the demons, showed extreme vanity with the thought that there was no one more powerful than them. They forgot that their success was due to Brahman's divine grace. In order to destroy their vanity, Brahman appeared before them as a Yaksha.

The devas did not know who the Yaksha was. They asked Agni to find out. The Yaksha placed a blade of grass before him, asking him to burn it. Agni used his power of burning, but failed. The devas sent Vayu next. With all his power, Vayu could not lift the blade of grass. Then Indra, the king of devas went to check himself, but the Yaksha had disappeared, and in his place stood Goddess Uma. She revealed the Yaksha's true identity as Brahman. She explained to Indra that all power emanated from one Great Power. That Power is Brahman. That Power is not seen or heard, or smelt. On the contrary, it is the Power by which man sees, hears and smells. Hence, the victory is not of manifested Self, but of Brahman.

Vajrasuchi Upanishad is about Vajrasuchi or the diamond needle that pierces ignorance, to cull out wisdom. It talks about being a brahmin. The soul is not a brahmin as it is the same in all beings. No single colour can characterise a brahmin. The body is also not the criteria as it is the same for everyone, being made up of the five elements. It does not depend upon birth either. Sage Rishyasringa was born of a deer, Kaushika of reed, Jambuka of a jackal, and Vyasa of a fisherwoman. They became brahmins on account of their knowledge. Karma is also not the mark of a brahmin because karma is found in all creatures. Only the one who has realised the Atman or Brahman, which is beyond knowledge, and which is realised by experience after prolonged meditation, can alone be called as a brahmin.

Maha Upanishad presents Vishnu as the highest being and describes the path to liberation and bliss as one of realising one's soul, of Brahman and Vishnu. The Upanishad states that a liberated person, a Jivanmukta, is characterised by one who is untouched by joy or grief, is free from desire, doesn't get angry, doesn't fear anyone, is an introvert, self-restrained, free from arrogance, envy and agitation.

Savitri Upanishad describes the Savitri Vidya, or the knowledge of Sunlight, declaring that everything in the universe is a manifestation of the masculine Savitar and feminine Savitri energies. Savitar is the creative energy and Savitri is the fuel and matter, both are interdependent and manifest together. They are linked to the Gayatri Mantra.

Aruneya Upanishad, also known as Sannyasa Upanishad, is one of the oldest renunciation related Upanishad. It is presented as a sermon given by Prajapati to Sage Aruni, where the former explains the character and lifestyle of a monk who has achieved the highest state of spirituality.

Maitreya Upanishad says that the wisest ones take up to contemplation of Brahman, the middle ones contemplate on scriptures, low people think of mantras and the lowest are deluded by the effectiveness of holy places. The worship of idols results in repeated births and deaths. Hence one should perform worship in one's heart only, contemplating on Brahman that is enshrined in one's heart, that is not different from the Self. The one who fully understands what is Brahman, without any delusion, the one who listens to this knowledge with supreme faith, merges in Brahman.

Kundika Upanishad is one of the Sannyasa Upanishads. It discusses when and how a person may take sannyasa. **Brihat-Sannyasa Upanishad** discusses how one has to enter into Sannyasa, the rites of renunciation, and how the sannyasi should live and behave. It identifies and describes six categories of monks, namely the Kutichaka, Bahudaka, Hamsa, Paramahamsa, Turiyatita and Avadhuta, in great details. The Upanishad also talks about who is entitled to renunciation, giving a manual-like list of those who do not qualify at all.

Vasudeva Upanishad is a dialogue between Lord Krishna also known as Vasudeva and Sage Narada, dedicated to the Vaishnava sacred tilak Urdhva Pundra. Krishna describes the tilak, explaining the importance of Gopichandana, the clay used to make it. The three vertical lines of Urdhva Pundra, pointing upwards, symbolise the Hindu trinity of Brahma, Vishnu and Shiva. **Avyakta Upanishad** explains how the universe evolved after creation. It says that no one is knowledgeable about its origin or whether it was framed by divine hand or not.

Rudraksha Upanishad is dedicated to Rudraksha, a seed used as prayer beads. The Upanishad is in the form of a conversation between Kalagni Rudra, a destructive form of Shiva and Sage Bhusunda, also known as Sanatkumara. The origin of Rudraksha, its different types, how to wear and the effects on the wearer, are discussed at length. Rudraksha was created from Shiva's tears.

Jabali Upanishad is a short Upanishad, structured as a discourse between Sage Jabali and Sage Pippalada. It states that all Jiva (living beings) are Pashu or animals in different forms. The Pati or Lord of all animals is Pashupati Shiva, the knower of everything. A Jiva lacks discrimination between the changing and the unchanging world, and is bothered by suffering and misery. The path to liberation starts by smearing our forehead with three horizontal lines of holy ash, remembering that everything will soon turn to ash. The lines represent the Rig, Yajur and Sama Vedas.

Maitrayani Upanishad asserts that the body is like a cart without intelligence. The reins are the five organs of perception, the steeds are the organs of action and the charioteer is the mind. The soul cannot be described. It is immortal, unmanifested, subtle, imperceptible, incomprehensible, selfless, pure, steadfast, stainless, desireless, fearless and self-abiding, and it dispels darkness. The elemental Self, due to ignorance on account of results of good and bad actions, does not comprehend the soul that is within its own self. By knowledge, yoga and meditation, God is realised and one attains union with the soul that is identical with various Gods and powers.

Yoga Choodamani Upanishad is called the Crown Jewel of Yoga. It presents the theory of Kundalini Yoga, chakras or the energy centres, nadis or the blood and energy vessels, prana the life force, and mudras. It asserts that enlightenment is achievable by combining Hatha Yoga, Kundalini Yoga and reflection on one's inner consciousness. It also claims that various illnesses of the body can be cured by asanas and breathing exercises.

Yoga Darshana Upanishad is in the form of a discourse given by Dattatreya to Sage Sankriti, based on a fusion of Hatha Yoga and Patanjali Yoga Sutras, on a foundation of Vedanta and Yoga philosophies. He asserts that God is within the temple of our body and the best pilgrimage is into our inner world, something we can do every day.

4

YAJUR VEDA AND ATHARVA VEDA

YAJUR VEDA

Yajur Veda is the book of rituals and contains the wisdom of sacrifices or yajna. Yajur comes from the root *yajus* meaning religious reverence, worship, a sacrificial prayer, particularly mantras uttered in a particular manner at a sacrifice. The Veda explains the yogic practices to be followed for purifying the mind and awakening the inner consciousness, the rituals for recreating the universe within oneself.

The most ancient layer of the Yajur Veda contains about 1,875 verses, out of which, 581 are from the Rig Veda.

The original Yajur Veda was taught by Vaishampayana to Yajnavalkya. Due to a misunderstanding, the disciple had to return the Veda to his guru. Yajnavalkya later invoked the Sun God and got knowledge again. This became known as the Shukla Yajur Veda. The earlier version taught by Vaishampayana became known as the Krishna Yajur Veda. Krishna means dark and Shukla means bright. The Krishna Yajur Veda deals with rituals, the explanations and directions incorporated within the text. The Shukla Yajur Veda contains only mantras necessary for the sacrifices, the explanations are given separately.

The **Krishna Yajur Veda** has three known Samhitas. They are: Taittiriya, Maitrayani, and Kathaka Samhitas. The Taittiriya Samhita is best known and deals with the detailed description of sacrifices like Agnishtoma, Jyothishtoma, Vajpeya, Rajasuya, and so on. It also talks about Surya Namaskar, and teaches mantras that are used to avert or cause havoc. The other Samhitas are not well-known, though they also deal with sacrifices.

In this Veda, the Brahmanas are not separate as they are appended to the Samhitas. Only two are available—Taittiriya and Vadhula Brahmanas—both appended to Taittiriya Samhita. There are three Aranyakas of Krishna Yajur Veda. They are: Taittiriya, Maitrayani and Kathaka Aranyakas for the three Samhitas.

Like the other Vedas, both the Yajur Vedas have several Upanishads in the concluding portions. There are 32 Upanishads attached to Krishna Yajur Veda.

Akshi Upanishad is a discourse from Sun-god Surya to Sage Samkriti. On the sage's request Surya teaches Brahma Vidya to him. The Ultimate Reality of the universe, the all-pervasive, infinite, Eternal Truth is called Brahman. To comprehend the true nature of Brahman, its relation to Self, is Brahma Vidya.

Amrita Bindu Upanishad discusses about the pure and impure mind. It says that the pure mind is without desires and the impure mind is with desires. The mind attached to sensual objects leads to bondage, while the mind that is devoid of attachments leads to liberation. Pure mind is needed for the one who seeks liberation. The Upanishad stresses that the Vedas are not only for reading, but for proper understanding and ultimate realisation of the Supreme Brahman.

Amrita Nada Upanishad asserts the need for the wise one to abandon all shastras after knowing the Brahman. It prescribes the practice the six limbs of Shadanga Yoga, which are: Pratyahara or subjugating the mind, Dhyąna or contemplation, Pranayama or control of breath, Dharana or concentration,

Dhyana or meditation and Samadhi or the state of bliss. It advises that to attain spiritual wisdom, one should avoid fear, anger, laziness, too much of sleep or lack of sleep, too much of food and fasting.

Avadhuta Upanishad describes the nature and characteristics of an Avadhuta, which means the liberated one. An Avadhuta has transcended discrimination by class or stage of life. He is driven by his Self (atman) alone, lives in bliss, wanders without care, and is unconcerned about his looks. He condemns all external sacrifices, performing them within himself. An Avadhuta is in union with God.

Brahma Upanishad deals with Hindu renunciation traditions. It starts with questions put up by a wealthy householder named Shaunaka to Sage Pippalada about the constitution of and the source of power in the human body, that he addresses as the 'divine city of Brahman'. Pippalada imparts the supreme wisdom of Brahman to Shaunaka. This Upanishad uses many analogies from nature, for example: just as a spider projects and withdraws the web by means of one thread, similarly Prana returns by drawing back.

Brahma Vidya Upanishad explains the structure of AUM, aspect of its sound, its placement, its beginning and end, and the significance of the fading away of the sound. AUM is Brahman, chanting which, the chanter becomes one with Brahman.

Dakshinamurti Upanishad opens with the prelude where some sages approach Sage Markandeya, asking him how he had managed to be a Chiranjeevi, the deathless one, and how he was always in a happy state. The sage answered that it was because of the knowledge of the most secret philosophy of Lord Shiva, who is Dakshinamurti, the one who at the time of the final deluge, keeps everything in himself and shines because of the bliss of his own spirit. The Upanishad ends by saying that one who reads and understands this secret philosophy of Shiva will get rid of all sins and will attain salvation.

Dhyana Bindu Upanishad says that Dhyana Yoga can destroy all the sins accumulated over many births. Nobody has been able to destroy their sins by any other method, dhyana or meditation is the only way to annihilate our sins. One can see God only through dhyana. The mind or the *manas* gets absorbed in the Supreme One only through dhyana. This Upanishad also describes Kundalini and how to awaken it.

Ekakshara Upanishad talks about AUM as the Ultimate Reality. The one immortal syllable *ekakshara* AUM is described as Hiranyagarbha, the golden egg, Brahma, manifested universe as well as the guardian of the universe. He is the love in all beings, the supporter, the imperishable, the source from which Vedas appeared, as well as the divinities and demons.

Garbha Upanishad points out that the body comprises the five elements of nature, namely, earth, water, fire, wind and ether. It then goes on to describe reproduction, the growth and development of a foetus until it gains complete human form in the eighth month, the birth of male and female babies and eunuchs, the qualities of parents at the time of impregnation which have effect on the child yet to be born, and also the birth of twins. The Upanishad asserts that the foetus has knowledge of its past lives, which it forgets during the process of birth. This Upanishad is considered a manual on human physiology.

Kaivalya Upanishad stresses the importance of renunciation for liberation or Kaivalya. It is presented as a conversation between Sage Ashvalayana and Lord Brahma, where the sage wants to learn Brahma Vidya or the knowledge of Brahman. The Upanishad unfolds through Brahma's discourse. He says that by meditating on Lord Shiva, who is ever peaceful, who is the source of all creation, who is the witness of all, and who is beyond all darkness, one gets liberated from rebirth, or attains the state of Kaivalya.

Kalagni Rudra Upanishad identifies Shiva as Brahman. *Kala-agni* is a composite of Rudra and Agni, meaning 'fire that is time'. It is a form of Shiva, one who creates everything from fire and then burns it all, gods, men and demons, to ashes. The Upanishad is a discourse by Kalagni Rudra (Shiva) to Sage Sanat Kumar on Tripundram, the three horizontal lines of sacred ash on the forehead. The lines symbolise the three sacred fires of household kitchen, holy fire lit in the south for our ancestors, and the fire of yajna, amongst other Hindu triads.

Kali Santarana Upanishad is a conversation between Lord Brahma and Sage Narada. *Kali-santarana* means 'crossing over discord'. At the end of Dwapar Yuga, Narada approached Brahma and requested him to show him the path to alleviate the detrimental effects of Kali Yuga. Brahma told Narada that by taking the name of the Supreme Deity Lord Narayana, all the tribulations of Kali Yuga will get washed away. He gave the mantra: 'Hare Rama, Hare Rama, Rama Rama, Hare Hare, Hare Krishna, Hare Krishna, Krishna Krishna, Hare Hare.' There are no rules for chanting this 16-word mantra.

Katha Upanishad tells the story of Nachiketa, the young son of Sage Vajasravasa, and the teachings imparted by Yama to Nachiketa. Though this Upanishad begins as a story, it leads to the exposition of the profound philosophical truths about the nature of man, Self, knowledge, and liberation. It is one of the most widely read and translated Upanishads, inspiring many philosophers across the world.

Kathashruti Upanishad is one of the Sannyasa Upanishads. It states that only after going through the first three stages of life, of studying the Vedas, getting married and raising a family, settling one's children in life, and retiring, should one take up sannyasa. Having decided to renounce, the renunciate should get cheerful approval from his wife, parents, and other family members. Then he should distribute his property and leave. The Upanishad further prescribes what kind of lifestyle a renunciate should have.

Kshurika Upanishad talks about the means to cut attachment using the knife of wisdom and shows the way to liberation. *Kshurika* means knife. The Upanishad discusses the importance of concentration of mind during meditation. It is mind only that can function as a *kshurika* or razor and cut away worldly distractions during Dhyana Yoga. The Upanishad also has chapters on asana, pranayama, and pratyahara, as a means to cleanse body and mind. The aim of Yoga, it says, is to know and liberate one's soul.

Mahanarayana Upanishad, despite its name, glorifies Narayana as well as Rudra, both as the first embodiment of Brahman, the metaphysical principle that existed before the creation of the Universe. In whom is the entire Universe and unto whom everything dissolves. The Lord of all creations envelops the whole space. In him, all creatures abide. He creates living beings out of the five elements. He enters into them as the inner controller, who is greater than the greatest, higher than the highest, the imperishable, and the one having unlimited forms.

Panchabrahma Upanishad glorifies Shiva as Sadashiva, as Brahman, with his five faces corresponding to five Ishvaras. The Upanishad describes the five forms of Reality (Pancha Brahman) that arose from the highest Reality. They are: Sadyojata, Aghora, Vamadeva, Tatpurusha and Ishana. Sadyojata represents earth and is associated with the power of action. Aghora represents fire and is associated with the power of desire. Vamadeva represents water and is associated with the power of knowledge. Tatpurusha represents air and is associated with the power of breath or life. Ishana represents ether or space and is associated with transcendence. These five forms of Reality are the Ishvaras represented by the five faces of Sadashiva.

Pranagnihotra Upanishad means sacrifice (hotra) offered to fire (agni) of life force (prana). The Upanishad says that the Universal Soul (God) is within our Self and all Vedic gods are embodied in the human body, giving us our various abilities. Eating food is like giving sacrifice to the gastric fire in the temple of our body. It further says that by doing Pranagnihotra, an internal spiritual rite, one becomes free from doing any external spiritual rites.

Rudrahridaya Upanishad presents Rudra (Shiva) and Uma as the Ultimate Reality of Brahman. It states that they are inseparable and together manifest as all gods and goddesses, all animals and inanimate reality of the universe. Everything in this universe is filled up with Rudra who is the masculine aspect, and Uma who forms the feminine aspect. The composite Rudra-Uma form is the Supreme Absolute, the AUM.

Sarasvati Rahasya Upanishad means the secret knowledge of the goddess of wisdom, Sarasvati. The Upanishad has two sections, the first consisting of hymns praising the goddess and seeking her blessings, and the second presenting a conversation between her and a devotee. Goddess Sarasvati is praised as the essence of truth, who manifests in anything that flows—words, music, voice, art, imagination—nourishing the mind and soul. Sarasvati herself states that even Brahma received eternal knowledge through her.

Sariraka Upanishad talks about the relationship between the elements of nature, human body and soul. The human body is mapped to its constitutional five elements: earth, water, fire, air and ether and their various attributes. Earth is connected to our bone, skin, nerves, hair and flesh. Water in our body can be seen in urine, phlegm, blood and semen. Fire is in hunger, thirst, laziness, delusion and sex. Air is in circulation, and movement of the eye. And ether is in lust, anger, greed, delusion and fear. The soul is the Lord of the body.

Sarvasara Upanishad defines and explains different concepts like bondage, liberation, ignorance etc. For example, the bondage or *bandhan* of the soul is the Self looking upon things other than itself and thinking them as itself. Moksha or liberation is the cessation of false idea of bondage. Avidya or ignorance is that which causes egoism, while vidya or knowledge is that by which egoism is eliminated.

Skanda Upanishad is narrated by Skanda (Kartikeya), the God of war and son of Lord Shiva. It emphasises that there is no difference between Vishnu and Shiva and all other gods. Skanda says that a living being or Jiva is Shiva. Just as before husking, rice is paddy, and after husking it's called rice grain, likewise, bound by karma is Jiva, liberated from it becomes the eternal Shiva.

Shukarahasya Upanishad is a discourse between Lord Shiva and Shuka, son of Sage Vyasa. Shiva teaches four sacred statements or Mahavakyas from the four Vedas as tools for meditation to Shuka. They are: Knowledge is Brahman. I am Brahman. You are Brahman. The Self is Brahman. The Upanishad asserts that anyone can achieve spiritual liberation by meditating on the four Mahavakyas, without doing any rituals, chanting mantras or going for pilgrimages.

Shvetashvatara Upanishad answers the metaphysical questions about the primal cause of all existence, its origin and end. It identifies the Supreme Brahman with Rudra (Shiva) who is the material and efficient cause of the world and its protector and guide. The emphasis here is not on Brahman, the Absolute or Impersonal God but on personal Ishvara who is omnipotent and omniscient and who is manifested as Rudra, who is the Superior Being. He is the Universal Soul who created this Universe, rules the world, protects and withdraws the world at the time of dissolution.

Taittiriya Upanishad lays down the rules of Brahmacharya or student life, its importance, about Vedic chanting and meditation on Pranava. It is divided into three sections. The first, Shikshavalli initiates a student into school and outlines the basic educational content, as well as conduct and responsibilities as a student. The second, Anandavalli focuses on the theme of Atma and Brahman, stressing that man reaches his highest potential and understands the deepest knowledge only by learning the right and unlearning the wrong. The last, Bhriguvalli shares the knowledge about Brahman that Sage Bhrigu received from his father Sage Varuni.

Tejobindu Upanishad is one of the most important Yoga Upanishads, expounded by Lord Shiva. It defines the 15 limbs of Yoga, describing the difficulties in achieving meditation and Samadhi and ways to overcome them. The Upanishad asserts that physical Yoga does not provide complete results unless the mind is purified by right knowledge and introspection. Instead of learning scriptures, it advises practice of meditation.

Varaha Upanishad is a sermon of the Varaha (boar) avatar of Vishnu to Sage Ribhu. He talks about Tattvas or aspects of reality that constitute human experience, the nature of and relationship between Atman and Brahman, the various stages of learning, the state of eternal bliss, the types of liberated persons and, the goals and methods of Yoga.

Yoga Kundalini Upanishad is one of the most important texts on Kundalini Yoga, extremely valuable in the Tantra (Shakti) tradition of Hinduism. The Upanishad states that the human mind, the source of behavioural tendencies, is influenced by memories and Prana. Balanced food, Yoga and arousing the inner power of Kundalini are recommended to master Prana. Further, the steps for Kundalini arousing are explained.

Yogashikha Upanishad is also called the crest of Yoga and discusses the role of Yoga in achieving moksha, or liberation while living. It considers AUM to be the mool-mantra (root mantra) and describes it as part masculine Shiva and part feminine Shakti and prescribes meditation on Atman, the Eternal Self and AUM. The Upanishad discusses different kinds of Yoga and says that the state of Pure Being is achieved only through the pursuit of knowledge and Yoga.

Yogatattva Upanishad is among the oldest known texts on Yoga that gives detailed description of Yoga techniques along with its benefits. It describes and compares the four types of Yoga: Mantra Yoga or practice through chants, Laya Yoga through deep concentration, Hatha Yoga through exertion and Raja Yoga through meditation. The Upanishad declares Yoga and knowledge to be mutually complementary and necessary. Not the scriptures, but knowledge of Ultimate Reality and Supreme Self, the Brahman, leads to the path of Self-realisation.

The Samhita in the **Shukla Yajur Veda** is called Vajasaneyi Samhita. It deals with major Vedic sacrifices in its 40 chapters. Some of the well-known sacrifices are: Pindapitrayajna to propitiate our forefathers, Rajasuya for a king's coronation, Vajapeya for warriors and kings, and Ashvamedha for sovereign kings. Apart from this, the Samhita also has mantras for magical rites, battle march, game of dice, and so on.

Two Brahmanas of Shukla Yajur Veda are available. They are Shatapatha and Kanva Brahmanas. Shatapatha means of hundred paths. **Shatapatha Brahmana** contains a hundred discourses discussing ceremonies and the philosophy of sacrifices. The Brahmana talks about Creation and recounts how Manu was warned by a fish whom he had helped, that a flood would destroy the entire humanity. It also gives elaborate explanations about the preparation of altars, ceremonial objects, ritual recitations, along with the symbolic attributes of each and every aspect of the Vedic sacrifices. The Kanva Brahmana consists of more than hundred discourses, some comprising discussions on metaphysical matter and others dealing with sacrificial rituals not usually practised.

The Aranyaka of Shukla Yajur Veda is **Brihad Aranyaka** and deals exclusively with Pravargya ritual, an introductory ceremony of Somayajna, which is conducted for the maintenance of cosmic order.

Shukla Yajur Veda has nineteen Upanishads attached to it.

Adhyatma Upanishad discusses the rejection of the identification with the world, body and shastras, destruction of mind by removing the superimposition of the feeling of 'I', disappearance of the mind with the knowledge of the Self by meditating and by dissolving the Self in the Supreme Self or Brahman. It describes the eternal form of Brahman and equates it with Lord Narayana (Vishnu). The Upanishad also dwells on the concept of Samadhi and how Vairagya (detachment) leads to Bodha (spiritual understanding).

Advayataraka Upanishad says that illusion (Maya) results in the differentiation of the living being from God. It talks about understanding and examining the illusion, with the knowledge of negation or Neti (not this, not that) realising the Advaya (nondual) Brahman. The Upanishad also speaks about the important role a guru plays in eliminating ignorance from his student's mind. The text includes Taraka Yoga, Raja Yoga and Kundalini Tantra and hence is also classified as a Yoga Upanishad.

Bhikshuka Upanishad describes four kinds of Sannyasi namely, Kutichaka, Bahudaka, Hamsa and Paramahamsa. Their path to spiritual liberation is through Yoga. The Kutichaka are saffron-clad hut-dwelling ascetics, carrying a three-pronged staff, who live on eight mouthfuls of food. The Bahudaka live in holy places near sacred waters and take eight mouthfuls of food as alms from the houses of brahmin sages. The Hamsa are those who stay only for one night for shelter in a village, five nights in a town, and seven nights or more in holy places. They live on cow's urine and other products from cows. The Paramahamsa are those who live under the shade of trees, deserted houses, or in cemeteries. They may or may not wear anything. They are wandering monks and seek shelter only for the night. They seek alms from anyone just for sustaining their life-breath.

Brihadaranyaka Upanishad is a treatise on Atman (Self). It states that the universe is made up of matter, energy, Atman and knowledge. It also claims that Atman and Brahman are the same. The Self is imperishable, invisible and pervades all of Reality. Hence, all organic beings are interconnected with each other and with Self. Inorganic nature is the field where the beings act. Both are mutually dependent, nourishing and nurturing each other, all stemming from one Self, the Brahman.

Hamsa Upanishad is a discourse between Sage Gautama and the divine Sanat Kumara, on Hamsa Vidya, a prelude to Brahma Vidya. Hamsa symbolises reincarnating soul. The Upanishad describes a tantra process to energise the chakras to meditate on Hamsa, the eight-petalled lotus in the heart. Once the person realises Brahman, the duality vanishes, his doubts and desires are destroyed, and he shines with inner calm and bliss.

Isha Upanishad is one of the shortest Upanishads. Isha means the Lord, the Self of all, our innermost Self, the one Absolute Reality. For liberation, we must know the Self, which though motionless is faster than wind, is distant yet near, is within all and outside all. We must behold all beings in Self and Self in all beings. The Upanishad teaches that sorrow and suffering cease to exist if we focus beyond our ego and understand that the Self is in all things. Once, this realisation comes, all things bring pleasure because then we begin to consider ourselves as an instrument of God. It is by renunciation and absence of possessiveness that the Self is liberated.

Jabala Upanishad says that anyone can renounce the world and become a sannyasi, regardless of which stage of life he is in. A true sannyasi is one who does not injure anyone in thought, word or deed, is without attachment to anyone or anything, abandons all rituals and is devoted to the oneness of Atman and Brahman. The Upanishad states that the true-Brahman seat of all beings is Avimuktam, the place that Shiva never left, the city of Kashi (Varanasi).

Mandala Brahmana Upanishad is taught by Narayana (Vishnu) to Sage Yajnavalkya, describing Yoga as a means to highest wisdom. Hence, it is also classified as one of the Yoga Upanishads. The text is structured as an eight-limb Yoga programme. It says that the mind influenced and controlled by worldly objects is the cause of bondage, and the one that isn't, is ready for spiritual liberation. The Upanishad asserts that it is our mind only that creates, preserves and destroys dissatisfaction.

Mantrika Upanishad says that if we see with eyes of knowledge, we will see Brahman everywhere. It is this Brahman in whom the universe is woven, including all that moves and does not move. It is Brahman from whom the material world emerges and into whom it finally merges. In our body, Brahman exists as soul, and this soul changes its dwelling thousands of times.

Muktika Upanishad is a dialogue between Lord Rama and Hanuman about Mukti or liberation. Rama states that Vedanta is his breath and explains about the four Vedas, each having Upanishads and states that even by reading one verse from the Upanishads with devotion one gets united with the Supreme. He further explains that amongst the different kinds of liberation, the only real type of liberation is Kaivalya or detachment. Rama advises Hanuman to practise the destruction of mental impressions and teaches him the importance of giving up cravings to become detached.

Niralamba Upanishad defines and explains Brahman, Jiva, Paramatma, Prakriti, Brahma, Vishnu, Rudra, Indra, Yama, Surya, Chandra, gods, demons, and evil spirits. It also talks about men, women, animals, knowledge, ignorance, pleasure, pain, heaven, hell, bondage, liberation, disciple, sage, austerity, and the supreme abode. It defines that which is sought after, that to be rejected, and the one who renounces, and so on. This Upanishad is like a glossary for the 108 Upanishads.

Paingala Upanishad describes the state of inner insight when one's sense of duality has disappeared, when Brahman is sensed within oneself as well as in everyone and everything. In this state the person is said to be liberated. Such a person needs no customs or rituals, as he has outgrown the world of illusion and has realised the Truth. The Upanishad asserts that what matters is Self-knowledge and not the holiness of the place where one lives or dies.

Paramahamsa Upanishad is a discourse between Lord Brahma and Sage Narada, primarily about the path and duties of a Paramahamsa Yogi. Brahma says that the path of a Paramahamsa lies in the ever-pure Brahman. He not only renounces his family and loved ones, but also the sacred thread, top-knot, rituals and recitations. Renouncer of all the worldly pleasures, he is immune to the existence of his body as well.

Shatyayaniya Upanishad, one of the Sannyasa Upanishads, asserts that the mind attached to sense objects is the cause of bondage and suffering, whereas the detached leads to liberation. It is the mind that shapes a person's future. To know the highest Truth, one must know Brahman. To do that, the mind has to be detached from the objects of senses and is to be focused on Brahman. The mind is everything; what you think, so you become. The Upanishad also talks about the four kinds of ascetics namely Kutichaka, Bahudaka, Hamsa and Paramahamsa.

Subala Upanishad is in the form of dialogue between Sage Subala and Prajapati about Vedic cosmogony. It states that the universe started from nothing, where neither spirit nor matter existed. In that nothingness existed Brahman, from which darkness emerged. From the darkness emerged ether, and from ether emerged air. From air emerged fire, from fire emerged water, and from water emerged earth. From earth emerged the egg, that split to create atmosphere and land, between which appeared the divine person, Purusha, who created death.

Tarasara Upanishad is a Mantra Upanishad and stresses the importance of AUM for yogic meditation as Taraka, that which helps one cross from the material to the spiritual world. The text describes its eight subtle sound elements: A, U, M, bindu, nada, kaal (present time), kalatita (future), and the last subtle sound that is beyond kalatita. The Upanishad maps these eight sound elements on the central characters of the *Ramayana*, as Jambavan, Sugriva, Hanuman, Shatrughna, Bharata, Lakshman, Sita, and Rama, respectively.

Trishikhibrahmana Upanishad is classified as one of the Yoga Upanishads, as most of its discussion is centred on the eight limbs of Yoga. It states that Yoga and knowledge are the ways to know Atman. Renunciation of karma leads to peace, but that happens only when one has acquired the right knowledge of Atman. The text also explains the theory of life and asserts that everything is Shiva, the Absolute, the one being that appears to be divided into many beings and matter.

Turiyatitavadhuta Upanishad is one of the Sannyasa Upanishads. It describes the nature and life of a self-realised monk or Turiyatita Avadhuta. Such a person does not perform any rituals or chant mantras. He feels no pain or pleasure, and fears nothing. He neither loves nor hates anyone. He eats if he finds something edible, or else he doesn't. He wanders alone. He understands and lives by the divine secret that 'there is no one different than me'. Such an Avadhuta is rare, says the Upanishad.

Yajnavalkya Upanishad is one of the Sannyasa Upanishads and describes the behaviour expected from a sannyasi who has renounced all social and material attachments. It gives reasons for the sannyasi to never desire women and children, in order to fulfil his vow to lead a celibate lifestyle. He must seek to perfect his own nature by renouncing anger too, as anger reveals one's own inner faults. The sannyasi is advised to see his own body as a source of internal sorrow, just like an enemy is a source of external sorrow.

ATHARVA VEDA

Atharva Veda is the last of the four Vedas. It is associated with the name of the ancient poet Atharvan, meaning 'the wise old one', hence is referred to as the Veda of the wise and old. This Veda is also associated with the name of another seer called Angirasa and therefore is also called the Atharvangirasa Veda. The Veda is dual in nature, dealing with sorcery on the one hand and Shanti Pushti rites on the other, which are associated with these two sages.

Atharva Veda has simpler language as compared to the other Vedas. It is a fusion of prose and poetry, and one-sixth of it is from Rig Veda.

The Atharva Veda Samhita is organised into 20 chapters or kands containing hymns of diverse nature. The hymns of this Veda contain lot of knowledge about the physical and material world, and spirituality. There are spells for destroying enemies, demons, wizards, harmful and poisonous animals like snakes, and also against those who oppress brahmins.

There are also hymns for positive effects like obtaining and ensuring love, happy family life, rituals for fulfilling one's desires, protection during journeys, building and construction, trade and commerce, statecraft, luck in gambling and things like that.

However, a major part of this Veda is concerned with human physiology, different ailments, their cure, and rituals for long life. The Atharva Veda is the first Indian text explaining diseases and medicines. There are verses identifying the cause of diseases, even leprosy, in the form of agents and the herbs to destroy these agents and cure the diseases. The verses glorify the curative powers of various medicinal plants and herbs, as well as water. They also elaborate on yoga and natural beauty. Ayurveda is considered as the Upa Veda of the Atharva Veda.

There are references of military practices and the associated kshatriya rites. A variety of devices such as an arrow with a duct for poison, poisoned nets, hook traps, use of disease spreading bugs, and smoke screens are explained in this Veda.

At the same time, one can also find highly philosophical ideas that are very close to the Upanishads. These verses are referred to as Siddha mantras.

The Atharva Veda does not have any Aranyaka, and its only surviving Brahmana is **Gopatha Brahmana**. There are two parts of this Brahmana—Purvardha and Uttarardha. The Purvardha glorifies Sage Atharvan and the related priests. Uttarardha contains critical appreciation of the rituals.

There are 31 Upanishads associated with Atharva Veda.

Annapurna Upanishad talks about fivefold delusions in this world. The first delusion is believing the living being (Jiva) to be separate from God. The second, equating the attribute of agency dwelling in the Self, as Self. The third, assuming Jiva as body. The fourth, assuming the cause of the universe to be changing. The fifth, presuming the unchanging Reality to be different from the cause of the universe. These delusions prevent us from understanding Self.

Atharvashikha Upanishad defines the meaning and importance of the divine mantra AUM, representing the

Ultimate Reality. The first syllable A represents earth (prithvi), Rig Veda, Brahma the creator, and the scared fire of the household. The second syllable U represents sky (akasha), Yajur Veda, Rudra the destroyer, and the ritual fire of the ancestors. The third syllable M represents heaven, Sama Veda, Vishnu the preserver, and the sacred fire of sacrifice. The fourth syllable, the hidden part that follows M, represents Atharva Veda, the Supreme Being (Purusha) and reverberates as the sound of Brahman.

Atharvashiras Upanishad is dedicated to Shiva as Rudra. It talks about Rudra being omniscient, omnipotent and omnipresent. Rudra is the innermost essence of all Reality, visible or invisible. He is Atman and Brahman. Through him the entire universe spreads out, says the text. Rudra is energy, he is AUM and the silence that follows AUM. Whoever knows him, enters peace. Rudra can be realised by abandoning worldly desires and through silence alone.

Atman Upanishad describes three types of Self or Atman. The external Self or Bahya-atma is the physical body that is born to die. The inner Self or Antar-atma is the individual soul that gets trapped in desires. The highest Self or Param-atma is Brahman. The text advises to meditate upon the highest Self through yoga, breath control, withdrawal from sense organs, contemplation and concentration. The knower of Brahman finally becomes one himself. For such a one, there is no rebirth.

Bhasmajabala Upanishad is a conversation between Sage Bhusunda Jabala and Lord Shiva about vibhuti or bhasma, the sacred ash, and rudraksha beads. The text describes the procedure of making bhasma, its purification and preservation, its smearing, where it should be applied, what mantras are to be recited at the time of its application, and which persons are fit for the recitation of mantras. The Upanishad also talks about the importance of the city of Varanasi, that one who dies there becomes one with Shiva.

Bhavana Upanishad identifies the human body as a Sri Yantra, comprising nine interlocking triangles embodying complex symbolism. It is one of the Shakta Upanishads, where the godhead or the metaphysical Reality is considered to be Goddess Shakti or Devi. The four upward triangles represent the masculine aspect of Devi, called Shiva, while the five downward triangles represent the feminine aspect of Devi, called Shakti. Symbolising the union of masculine and feminine energies, the Yantra itself represents the totality of the cosmos with the cosmic centre, called Bindu as the power point. This Bindu is Shakti. The Upanishad focuses on internal worship as opposed to external rituals.

Brihajjabala Upanishad is presented as a conversation between Sage Bhusunda and Kalagni Rudra where the latter talks about five types of sacred ash and their association with Shiva. Vibhuti is associated with the Sadyojata form of Shiva and the element earth. Bhasita is associated with Vamadeva form of Shiva and the element water. Bhasma is associated with Aghora form of Shiva and the element fire. Kshara is associated with Tatpurusha form of Shiva and the element air. Raksha is associated with Ishana form of Shiva and the element ether. The text discusses the various merits of using the sacred ash.

Dattatreya Upanishad prescribes that one should meditate on Vishnu in the form of Dattatreya to free oneself from the cycle of birth-death-rebirth. The Upanishad presents one, six, eight, twelve and sixteen-syllable mantras and the mukti mantra of Dattatreya, describing him as the manifestation of all mantras, tantras and powers. The text says that Dattatreya is easily pleased by simply remembering him, and his blessings fulfil all the wishes in a devotee's heart and bring great joy to the mind.

Devi Upanishad states that Devi is the fountainhead of all mantras, the ultimate metaphysical Reality, and it is from her that matter (Prakriti) and consciousness (Purusha) arise. She is bliss and non-bliss, knowledge and ignorance, Vedas and non-Vedas, born and unborn, below, above and around, basically the universe in its entirety. Devi represents all gods, demons, ghosts, evil beings, super beings, planets, stars, and even time and its divisions. She is everything that was, is, and will be in the universe. The Upanishad explains the greatness of worshipping Devi.

Ganapati Upanishad starts with the worship of Ganapati or Lord Ganesha as the creator, maintainer, destroyer, the Supreme Principle Brahman. It equates Ganesha with Brahma, Vishnu, Shiva, all deities, the universe and AUM. The text says that one who meditates on Lord Ganapati knowing that he is the Supreme, becomes a yogi above all yogis, that one who studies this Upanishad, moves towards Brahman and is always blissful, not bound by obstacles.

Garuda Upanishad is dedicated to Garuda, who is the eagle-mount of Lord Vishnu, and an eternal enemy of the snakes. It has mantras to neutralise all kinds of poisons, whether from poisonous animals and insects, or even poisonous arrows. Sage Bharadwaj taught the Upanishad to his disciples. The sage was well known for his spells to prevent and cure infectious diseases, wounds caused by weapons or wild beasts, infestations by insects and worms, and snakebite. The text claims that one who teaches this great knowledge to a thousand brahmins is able to remove snake poison by means of his thought alone.

Gopala Tapani Upanishad focuses on Gopala or Lord Krishna as the Supreme Personality, whom death feared and who created the universe. The text describes spiritual practices leading to the realisation of Krishna being the Highest Truth. It also contains an account of Radha as Krishna's principal consort, hence making it a significant scripture for Radha worshippers.

Hayagriva Upanishad is dedicated to Hayagriva, the horse-headed avatar of Lord Vishnu, and presents mantras to know the nature of the Supreme Reality, Brahman. The text asserts that one who masters the mantras of Hayagriva, learns the wisdom of the scriptures, Shruti, Smriti, Itihasa and Purana, and is blessed with prosperity. The Upanishad claims Hayagriva to be the manifestation of Rig Veda, Sama Veda, Yajur Veda and AUM, the ruler of knowledge, and the teacher of humanity.

Krishna Upanishad narrates how Lord Rama was born as Lord Krishna and how various divinities and virtues became people and objects in his life. Mother Earth, mercy, humility, sense-control, truth, and broken curd pots were born as Rohini, Satyabhama, Sudama, Sage Uddhava, Sage Akrura and the ocean of milk respectively. Sage Kashyapa was the mortar and Goddess Atri became the rope with which Lord Krishna was tied. The harvest season became the meals in the house and the lotus that the Lord held became the seed of the world. Thus, Vaikuntha of the heaven was brought down to earth.

Mahavakya Upanishad describes the nature of Self and Brahman, asserting that they are one. It says that the state of liberation is the state of full understanding of this oneness. The text says that Vedic rituals and chasing sensual pleasures is a sign of darkness within. The way to shed this darkness is to practise introspection and yoga. The spiritual knowledge that one attains from it, brings about the radiance of Self-discovery.

Mandukya Upanishad declares that the symbol AUM is Brahman, the entire universe. It further explains the principle of AUM in context with the four states of consciousness, namely wakeful, dreaming, dreamless sleep and transcendental consciousness, which is the all-inclusive and ultimately the real state. The first three are associated with the three syllables of AUM, and fourth is the silence of the ardhmatra. In the waking state one enjoys all gross objects. In the state of dream, one is inwardly conscious and enjoys the subtle objects. In the state of dreamless sleep, everything is absorbed and there are no desires or dreams, one gets unified with consciousness and full bliss. The fourth state, beyond dreamless sleep is the transcendental stage. It is beyond all thought, duality and beyond knowing. One who knows all these stages enters Self.

Mundaka Upanishad teaches the distinction between the higher knowledge, the Supreme Brahman, and the lower knowledge of the material world. It claims that only by higher wisdom and not by sacrifices or worship can one realise Brahman. The lower knowledge is knowledge of the Veda and Smriti like Vedanga namely, phonetics, grammar, logic, history, rituals, astrology, and so on. The higher knowledge is the knowledge of the imperishable, formless all-pervasive Brahman. The one who realises this Brahman becomes Brahman himself. As rivers ultimately flow or merge into the ocean, similarly the liberated soul merges with Brahman, that is God.

Naradaparivrajaka Upanishad is one of the Sannyasa Upanishads and explores the spiritual path of renunciation and the monastic life. It provides detailed guidance on the lifestyle, duties, and practices of monks and renunciates. The Upanishad emphasises detachment from worldly desires and material possessions as the foundation for spiritual growth and enlightenment. It instructs the seeker to cultivate self-discipline, devotion, and meditation. Central to its teachings is the pursuit of Brahman and achieving Moksha or liberation from the cycle of birth and death.

Nrisimha Tapaniya Upanishad is dedicated to the deity Nrisimha (Narasimha), an avatar of Vishnu. This Upanishad is split into two sections: the Purva or former and the Uttara or latter. It explores the mystical and philosophical significance of the Naraṣimha maṇtra and the form of the deity as half-man, half-lion. The text delves into the nature of reality, the power of devotion, and the path to liberation through meditation on Narasimha. Emphasising on the protection and blessings of the deity, it serves as a guide for spiritual seekers aspiring to overcome fear and ignorance.

Parabrahma Upanishad elaborates on the nature of Parabrahma, the Supreme and Ultimate Reality, as the source of all existence, beyond time and space, and without form or attributes. It delves into the idea of the Self as identical to this Supreme Reality, encouraging one to transcend the limitations of the physical and mental planes. The text emphasises the importance of meditation and knowledge in realising this truth and encourages abandoning the external rituals. It also discusses the dissolution of individual identity into the cosmic consciousness to achieve liberation.

Paramahamsa Parivrajaka Upanishad is a Sannyasa Upanishad. It is a treatise on the life and conduct of Paramahamsa, ạ monk of the highest order in monastic traditions. It describes the ideal characteristics of such a monk, including humility, compassion, purity of mind, and an unwavering focus on the divine. He bows to none, does not worship any god, and is above all rules and duties of the world. A Paramahamsa accepts food and water from anyone without discrimination. The text emphasises the realisation of the Self as identical with the Ultimate Reality Brahman and provides guidelines for those on the path of spiritual liberation through devotion and meditation.

Pashupatabrahma Upanishad is dedicated to the worship and understanding of Lord Shiva as Pashupati, the Lord of all beings. The Upanishad emphasises the symbolic significance of Lord Shiva's attributes, such as his matted hair and ash-smeared body, as representing deeper spiritual truths. It guides practitioners on achieving liberation through meditation, self-control, and the renunciation of worldly attachments. The Upanishad asserts that by having discipline in food habits, mental discipline develops, which eventually leads to wisdom that solves all problems. The one who sees Brahman in everything sees Brahman in himself.

Prashna Upanishad is in the form of six questions posed by six disciples of Sage Pippalada. Each question addresses fundamental aspects of existence and spiritual knowledge. Topics include the origin of life, nature of Prana the vital force, role of the mind and senses, importance of meditation and the Ultimate Reality of Brahman. The sage provides detailed explanations, using metaphors and analogies to illustrate complex concepts. The Upanishad concludes that Self-knowledge, the knowledge of Brahman, is the highest knowledge.

Rama Rahasya Upanishad delves into the mystical and spiritual significance of Lord Rama, considered an embodiment of the Ultimate Reality or Brahman. The text is presented as a conversation between Hanuman and many sages seeking true knowledge, where the former reveals the importance of chanting Rama's name and meditating on his divine form. The text discusses many Rama mantras that grant protection and liberation. It highlights the transformative power of devotion to Rama, leading to self-realisation and enlightenment. The Upanishad claims that by understanding the hidden truth (rahasya) within the mantras, one can achieve unity with Brahman.

Rama Tapaniya Upanishad is dedicated to the worship of Lord Rama as a form of the Supreme Reality, Brahman. Divided into two parts, the Purva and Uttara Tapaniya, the Upanishad explores Rama's attributes and spiritual significance. It discusses the significance of Rama mantra and Rama yantra, as well as the practice of meditation on Rama. The text portrays Rama not just as a historical or mythical figure, but as the essence of Ultimate Reality and inner peace, advocating devotion to Rama as a means to attain liberation and eternal bliss.

Shandilya Upanishad is attributed to Sage Shandilya and focuses primarily on the practice and philosophy of yoga. It provides detailed instructions on the eightfold path of Ashtanga Yoga, which includes ethical disciplines (yama), personal observances (niyama), physical postures (asana), breath control (pranayama), withdrawal of senses (pratyahara), concentration (dharana), meditation (dhyana), and absorption (samadhi). The Upanishad emphasises the importance of mental and spiritual discipline to achieve Self-realisation and liberation, declaring Self and Brahman to be the same.

Sharabha Upanishad focuses on Sharabha, a mythological eight-legged creature that combines the traits of lion, eagle, and man, and is considered a powerful manifestation of Shiva. The Upanishad presents the dialogue between Lord Narayana and Sage Ribhu, detailing the might of Sharabha as a form taken by Shiva to subdue the ferocity of Narasimha, the man-lion avatar of Vishnu. It symbolises the victory of higher spiritual forces over primal instincts and stresses the idea that Ultimate Reality transcends all forms and conflicts.

Sita Upanishad centres on Sita, the wife of Lord Rama. It describes Sita as primordial nature or Prakriti, as the material cause behind all manifestation. The Upanishad portrays Sita as the Shakti or divine energy of Rama and explores her virtues and spiritual significance. Through narratives and philosophical dialogues, it highlights her role in the cosmic order and her importance in the path to liberation. Sita personifies the goddess of prosperity Lakshmi, mother earth Bhudevi and the goddess of destruction Durga. She is the Supreme Goddess, the Atman that resides in all beings.

Surya Upanishad is dedicated to Surya the Sun God, the creator, protector and destroyer of the universe. The Upanishad elaborates the spiritual and yogic significance of Surya as the Ultimate Reality, light, and life-giving force. It also includes the Surya Gayatri Mantra, extolling the Sun as the illuminator of the mind and soul. The text advocates worship and meditation on Surya for health, prosperity, and enlightenment. It discusses the importance of the sun in sustaining the universe and describes rituals and practices to harness solar energy for spiritual growth and liberation.

Tripadvibhuti Mahanarayana Upanishad focuses on the concept of Tripad-vibhuti, describing the three-fold glory of Lord Narayana, representing the entirety of the cosmos. It elaborates on the different dimensions of his divine presence: the manifest, the unmanifest, and the transcendental. Through hymns and verses, the Upanishad emphasises devotion to Narayana as a path to achieving supreme knowledge and unity with the divine.

Tripuratapini Upanishad is a Shakta Upanishad presenting Goddess Tripura as the Supreme Goddess and an embodiment of the universal mother, the primordial power. It elaborates on the nature of Tripura as the ultimate reality and consciousness, transcending and immanent in the cosmos. The Upanishad explores the esoteric knowledge associated with her worship, including the sacred mantras and the mystic yantras used in meditation. It emphasises on achieving liberation through devotion, meditation, and understanding of the goddess, representing the unity of the divine feminine and the cosmos.

5

UPANISHAD OR VEDANTA

The Upanishad represent the final understanding of the mystic sense of the Veda. They answer questions on the origin of the universe, the nature of God, the nature of soul and the connection between mind and matter. They are known as the Vedanta, meaning the end of the Veda. They are the beginning of the metaphysical inquiry, which resulted in the development of Hindu philosophy.

Upanishads are in the form of philosophical stories, dialogues, discourses, arguments, discussions, chants or hymns, dealing with nature of reality, individual soul and the universal soul. They begin with profound questions like: who directs the mind to go towards objects? What power directs the eyes and ears? There are questions about where we came from, how life is manifested in us, and so on. The questions are put by earnest students sitting close to their teacher or guru's feet. The word *Upanishad* is derived from *upa* (by) and *ni-shad* (sit down), referring to the student sitting down near the teacher.

There is no reference to any religion or system of philosophy, and no rituals or worship of any gods.

In the Upanishads, there is only one real Existence in the universe, the Supreme Brahman, Universal Soul, Paramatma or Self and all the creatures are manifestations of this Self. Brahman comes from the root *brih,* meaning vast, expansive and all-pervasive. It is the source from which the world originated, that in which the world exists, and into which the world dissolves. Brahman is the One Being of the very nature of Consciousness and Love, where Being implies Existence (sat), Consciousness gives Knowledge (chit), and Love (ananda) gives Bliss. Sat-Chit-Ananda is a way to describe Brahman, as is Satyam-Jnanam-Anantam or Truth-Knowledge-Infinity.

The recurring theme of the Upanishads is that Brahman can be realised here and now by earnest aspirants, and that this realisation makes one blissful and free from the cycle of birth and death.

The doctrine taught is, you are a part of the Universal Soul, I am a part of the Universal Soul, we are all of the Divine. The individual soul known as Atman is the same as Brahman. Everything is based on the Law of Karma or cause (action) and effect. You reap what you sow. If your action is bad, its effect will also be bad. Therefore, you must be reincarnated until your activity is on the spiritual plane, which means your actions will be from the spiritual thought world. Once you reach that plane, rebirth is not necessary, because you will be absorbed into the divine essence. This is called Self-realisation. And Self is Brahman.

Unlike the voluminous Samhitas and Brahmanas, the Upanishads are short. Around 108 Upanishads are known, 10 of Rig Veda, 16 of Sama Veda, 19 of Shukla Yajur Veda, 32 of Krishna Yajur Veda and 31 of Atharva Veda. *(All of them are described in the chapters on their respective Vedas.)*

The Upanishads are loosely classified into Mukhya, Samanya, Shaiva, Vaishnava, Shakta, Yoga and Sannyasa Upanishads, but all of them primarily teach the practical means of realising Brahman, the ultimate and eternal truth. They show that through meditation, the ultimate truth or reality becomes the living reality, and the difference between individual Self and universal Self melts away. In the state, when one's individual Self dissolves or merges with Brahman, one becomes a sannyasi, and fully understands the four *mahavaakyas* or great mantras of the Upanishads, that form the basic principle of Hinduism.

The first mantra is *Prajnanam Brahman,* stated in Aitareya Upanishad of the Rig Veda. It means Consciousness is Brahman, that is, through our innermost, supreme and divine intelligence, we can merge with the supreme Brahman.

The second is *Aham Brahmasmi,* stated in the Brihadaranyaka Upanishad of the Yajur Veda. It means, I am Brahman or Consciousness, that is, God is in me (us) and not outside of me (us).

The third is *Tat Tvam Asi,* stated in the Chandogya Upanishad of the Sama Veda. It means, the Paramatma and you are one and the same.

The fourth is Ayam Atma *Brahman,* stated in Mandukya Upanishad of the Atharva Veda. It means, this soul or Self is Brahman, that is, I am the *Jeevatma* which is the spark of *Paramatma.*

The direct revelations of realisations of the sages in higher states of consciousness can also be replicated by earnest aspirants. The teachings of the Upanishads do not require any prior belief in Hinduism. A questioning mind and an interest in knowing the truth is all that is needed.

Some popular verses from the Upanishads

Asato Ma Sadgamaya
Tamaso Ma Jyotirgamaya
Mrtyorma Amritam Gamaya
Om Shantih Shantih Shantih

From untruth lead us to truth. From darkness lead us to light. From death lead us to immortality. Om peace, peace, peace. (Brihadaranyaka Upanishad)

Kama Maya Evayam Purusha Iti
Sa Yatha Kama Bhavati Tat Kratur Bhavati
Yat Kratur Bhavati Tat Karma Kurute
Yat Karma Kurute Tad Abhisam Padyate

You are what your deep, driving desire is. As your desire is, so is your will. As your will is, so is your deed. As your deed is, so is your destiny. (Brihadaranyaka Upanishad)

Yo Vai Bhuma Tat Sukham Nalpe Sukhamasti Bhumaiva Sukham

That which is infinite is the source of happiness. There is no happiness in the finite. Happiness is only in the infinite. (Chandogya Upanishad)

Na Jayate Mriyate Va Vipascin Nayam Kutascinna Babhuva Kascit
Ajo Nityah Sasvatoyam Purano Na Hanyate Hanyamane Sarire

The Self is never born, nor does it die. It did not originate from anything and nothing originates from it. It is unborn, eternal, abiding and primeval. It is not slain when the body is slain. (Katha Upanishad)

Anando Brahmeti Vyajanat
Anandadhyeva Khalvimani Bhutani Jayante
Anandena Jatani Jivanti
Anandam Prayantyabhisam Visantiti

Bliss is Brahman. From bliss beings are born. By bliss, when born, they live. Into bliss they enter at their death. (Taittiriya Upanishad)

6

SMRITI OR DHARMA SHASTRA

Shruti or the Veda were the first Hindu scriptures. Whatever scriptures came after them were collectively known as Smriti. The word *smriti* means 'that which is remembered'. The Smriti texts include the Purana, Itihasa, Vedanga, Upa Veda, and so on.

Eighteen major texts are explicitly called Smritis. They are: Manu, Yajnavalkya, Parashara, Vishnu, Daksha, Samvarta, Vyasa, Harita, Shatatapa, Vashishtha, Yama, Apasthamba, Gautuma, Devala, Shankha-Likhita, Usanana, Atri and Shaunaka Smritis. The well-known ones are the Manu, Yajnavalkya and Parashara Smritis. Of these, Manu Smriti is considered to be the oldest.

These texts are also called the Dharma Shastras or law books, since they describe the various religious and social laws and norms that guide individuals and communities in their daily conduct during different stages of evolution of society. Dharma refers to the law that holds together our conduct. They are said to be contextual truths rather than eternal truths.

As times change, the Smritis relevant to that particular age also change. Manu Smriti was relevant for Satya Yuga. Yajnavalkya Smriti was for Treta Yuga or the time of the *Ramayana*. Shankha-Likhita Smriti was for Dvapara Yuga or the time of the *Mahabharata*. Parashara Smriti is relevant for Kali Yuga or the present age.

The main topics dealt with in the Dharma Shastras include, dharma, karma, yajna, caste system, marriage and other rites, four stages of life, rules of eating, rules for celebrating festivals, pilgrimage vows, rules of renunciation, duties of a king, legal procedures, categories of sins and penances, propitiatory rites, ancestral rites and the rites for the dead.

Manu Smriti is the most important and the most popular of all the Dharma Shastras. It is also known as Manava Dharmashastra. It is in the form of a discourse by Sage Manu on the codes of law given to him by Lord Brahma. There are 2,031 verses in it.

Civil laws, laws of state, punishments, social obligations, daily duties, conquest of senses, study of scriptures, education, honouring the older people, respecting parents, are some of the major topics dealt with at great length in Manu Smriti.

It deals with cosmogony or the origin of the universe, dharma or the proper way of life and conduct, the samskaras or rituals like the sacred thread ceremony, marriage, funeral rites, pollution and purification. It extols virtues such as non-injury, truth, compassion, forbearance, moderation, and so on. It discusses rules governing charity and other good actions, karma and liberation. Rules for war say that non-combatants, civilians, women and those who surrender should not be harmed. It outlines a hierarchical social order, emphasising the duties and responsibilities of individuals based on their caste and stage of life.

Yajnavalkya Smriti is attributed to Sage Yajnavalkya, a renowned Vedic scholar. This text holds a significant place in the development of Hindu law and ethics. Unlike Manu Smriti, which is more rigid and prescriptive, Yajnavalkya Smriti is known for its pragmatic and relatively progressive approach.

The Smriti is divided into three main sections: Achara (conduct), Vyavahara (legal procedure), and Prayashchita (penance).

The Achara section deals with the duties of individuals according to their caste and stage of life. However, it also provides a more flexible interpretation of social duties, allowing for adaptations based on circumstances.

The Vyavahara section is noteworthy for its detailed legal codes, covering civil, criminal, and procedural law. It emphasises the importance of fairness and justice in legal proceedings and introduces concepts like the validity of contracts, the rights of women and property, and the duties of kings in governance.

The Prayashchita section deals with the expiation of sins, outlining various forms of atonement for different types of transgressions.

Yajnavalkya Smriti is often praised for its balanced and realistic approach to social and legal issues, making it a more adaptable and enduring legal text compared to Manu Smriti. It has been influential in shaping Hindu law, particularly during the medieval period.

Shankha-Likhita Smriti is attributed to sages Shankha and Likhita. Though not very well-known, this Smriti holds a unique place in the corpus of Dharma Shastra due to its detailed and practical approach to law and morality.

The Smriti is particularly recognised for its emphasis on judicial procedures and the administration of justice. It offers a detailed account of legal practices, including the roles of judges, the importance of evidence, the classification of crimes, and the corresponding punishments. This focus on legal matters indicates that the text was likely intended for practical use by rulers, judges, and administrators in ancient Indian society.

In addition to legal guidelines, the Smriti also addresses social and ethical norms, emphasising the importance of personal integrity, truthfulness, and adherence to one's prescribed duties.

Though not as widely studied as other Smritis, the Shankha-Likhita Smriti is valued for its clarity and systematic approach to law and ethics. It provides insight into the legal and moral thinking of ancient India, contributing to the broader understanding of Hindu jurisprudence and societal norms.

Parashara Smriti is attributed to Sage Parashara, the great-grandfather of the Kauravas and the Pandavas. This Smriti stands out among the Dharma Shastra for its adaptability and progressive stance on various social and religious issues, making it particularly relevant during the Kali Yuga, the current age according to Hindu cosmology.

One of the distinguishing features of the Smriti is its recognition of the changing nature of society and its willingness to adapt dharma (righteous duty) to the times. Parashara himself declares that his code is intended for the Kali Yuga, an age characterised by moral decline and societal challenges. This acknowledgment allows for a more flexible interpretation of laws and duties, differing from the rigid prescriptions found in older texts like Manu Smriti.

The text addresses topics such as social duties, legal procedures, penance, and religious observances. Notably, Parashara Smriti offers more lenient rules regarding the treatment of women and lower castes, reflecting a shift towards greater inclusivity. It also places significant emphasis on the concept of Ahimsa (non-violence) and the importance of ethical conduct in personal and communal life.

Parashara Smriti has been influential in shaping the legal and ethical discourse within Hinduism, especially in its more flexible and humane approach to social norms. Its relevance endures, particularly in contexts where tradition meets modernity, offering a model for interpreting dharma in a way that is both respectful of ancient wisdom and responsive to contemporary realities.

7
PURANA

Purana are a rich and expansive genre of ancient Hindu literature, playing a crucial role in the preservation and dissemination of religious and cultural knowledge. They were not composed at a single point in time; they existed in oral form before being written down, evolving over centuries. The Puranas are written in Sanskrit but have been translated into many languages over the centuries, allowing their teachings to reach diverse populations.

The word *purana* translates to 'ancient' or 'old', but these texts are more than mere historical accounts; they are encyclopaedic compilations that encompass mythology, cosmology, genealogies, theology, philosophy, and folklore. They are commentaries on the Veda and Upanishad, simplifying them using stories, for the ease of understanding by people. Composed in the form of narratives, they are often structured as dialogues between a sage and a disciple, which makes them accessible to a wide audience.

The Puranic accounts of creation of the universe are a blend of more than one theme. It could be the awakening of Vishnu to start the creative process, or a primal egg containing the universe or the dual principles of Prakriti (female) and Purusha (male) interacting or maybe the anthropomorphic body itself of God giving rise to different forms of life. However, one important thing to remember is that the cosmos that comes into existence from wherever also dissolves back into it; creation becomes re-creation. It's a cycle that has no beginning and will have no end.

The Puranas glorify Brahman in the form of godheads Brahma, Vishnu and Shiva. Of the Vedic gods, Indra, Agni, Soma, Vayu and Surya appear in the texts. There are numerous supernatural characters also in them, including the dead ancestors, celestial singers and dancers, and the gods and demons who are at constant war with each other.

Traditionally, there are 18 Maha Puranas (major Puranas) and 18 Upa Puranas (minor Puranas), each with its unique focus and narrative style. The difference between a Maha Purana and Upa Purana is that the former is well known, and the latter isn't. There are hundreds of other Puranas too, including those restricted to particular places called Sthal Puranas or to particular communities called Jati Puranas.

The Maha Puranas are Brahma, Padma, Vishnu, Shiva (or Vayu), Bhagavata, Naradiya, Markandeya, Agni, Bhavishya, Brahmavaivarta, Linga, Varaha, Skanda, Vamana, Kurma, Matsya, Garuda and Brahmanda Puranas.

The lengths of the Puranas vary enormously. An average length of a Purana is around 20,000 couplets. But, with 9,000 couplets, Markandeya Purana is the shortest. And with 81,100 couplets, Skanda Purana is the longest.

The Upa Puranas are Sanat Kumara, Narasimha, Brihan Naradiya, Shiva Rahasya, Durvasa, Kapila, Vamana, Bhargava, Varuna, Kalika, Samba, Nandikeshvara, Surya, Parashara, Vasishtha, Devi Bhagavata, Ganesha, and Hamsa Puranas.

Each Purana typically has five primary features or subjects, known as Panchalakshana: the creation of the universe (Sarga), its destruction and recreation (Pratisarga), genealogies of gods and sages (Vamsha), the reigns of the Manus, the legendary progenitors of humanity (Manvantara), and the history of royal dynasties (Vamsanucharita).

Beyond these, the Puranas delve into a wide array of topics, including the moral and ethical teachings, the rites and rituals of daily worship, descriptions of sacred places, festivals, and the stories of divine incarnations (avatars).

Since the Hindu triad Brahma-Vishnu-Shiva is very important, each Purana emphasises on it. But the degree of emphasis varies. Accordingly, Puranas that emphasise on creation are identified with Brahma: Brahma, Brahmaṇda, Brahmavaivarta, Markandeya, Bhavishya and Vaman Puranas.

Puranas that emphasise on Vishnu and his incarnations are identified with Vishnu: Vishnu, Naradiya, Bhagavata, Garuda, Padma and Varaha Puranas. Finally, Puranas that emphasise on norms and rituals are identified with Shiva: Matsya, Kurma, Linga, Shiva, Skanda, Agni and Vayu Puranas. All the major Puranas contain sections on Devi, the significant ones being Markandeya, Shiva, Linga, Brahmavaivarta, Agni and Padma Puranas.

Bhagavata Purana is particularly revered, known for its profound devotion to Lord Krishna and its philosophical teachings on the nature of reality. Markandeya Purana is revered for containing the Devi Mahatmya, a text central to Shakti worship that glorifies the Goddess as the supreme power.

In addition to their religious significance, the Puranas also serve as vital sources for understanding ancient Indian culture, history, geography, and social norms. They offer insights into the development of Hinduism, documenting the evolution of rituals, temple worship, and the worship of deities over time.

From the list we can see that the total number of Puranas is 19. This is because, as discovered by the eleventh century

Persian scholar Al Biruni, there are two lists, one containing Shiva Purana and no Vayu Purana, while the other has Vayu Purana but does not include Shiva Purana. So, if both these are accepted, then the Puranic genre has 19, not 18, major Puranas.

Skanda Purana claims that Shiva and Vayu Puranas are the same and the list should be of 18 Puranas only. However, further studies by scholars showed both the Puranas to be different. Hence, all 19 of them are described below.

Brahma Purana is often referred to as the Adi Purana due to its association with Brahma, the creator. It is a significant compilation that blends mythology, religious teachings, and geographical descriptions. The text is structured as a dialogue between Sage Suta and a group of rishis in the Naimisha forest, which is a common narrative style in Puranic literature.

The Purana covers an extensive range of topics, including the creation of the universe, the genealogies of gods, sages and kings, and stories of prominent deities like Vishnu, Shiva and Devi. A unique aspect of this Purana is its emphasis on Sun-god Surya. It extols the significance of Surya worship and details the construction, rituals, and importance of Surya temples, particularly the famous Konark Sun Temple in Odisha.

Additionally, the Purana offers guidance on various pilgrimages, with detailed accounts of sacred sites like Puri in Odisha, and others in the southern regions of India. It also delves into the stories of ancient kings like Prithu and the virtues of performing rituals like Shraadh for ancestors. The Brahma Purana is a rich source of Hindu religious, cultural, and historical knowledge, intertwining divine myths with practical instructions for worship and righteous living.

Padma Purana is named after *padma* (lotus), which is a symbol of purity and creation. The text is divided into five major sections or Khandas: Srishti (creation), Bhumi (earth), Swarga (heaven), Patala (netherworld), and Uttara (later section) Khandas. Together, these sections comprise over 55,000 verses, making it one of the longest Puranas.

The Purana is particularly noted for its emphasis on the practice of bhakti (devotion) towards Lord Vishnu, although it also gives significant attention to the worship of Shiva and the Goddess (Shakti), reflecting the inclusive and diverse nature of Hindu worship. It narrates various stories of Vishnu's incarnations, including the popular tales of Rama and Krishna, alongside detailed descriptions of holy sites (tirthas) and sacred rivers Ganga, Yamuna, and Saraswati.

A unique aspect of this Purana is its detailed descriptions of the rites, rituals, and festivals to be observed by devotees. It offers guidance on the performance of daily duties, the significance of pilgrimage, and the benefits of reading and hearing sacred texts. The Purana also includes narratives that promote ethical living and righteousness (dharma), often using allegorical tales to convey moral lessons.

Furthermore, Padma Purana is known for its elaborate eulogy of the Bhagavad Gita, underscoring its importance as a spiritual guide. It also highlights the glory of Tulsi (the sacred basil plant), which is revered in Hindu tradition as an embodiment of purity and devotion.

Vishnu Purana is a key text for the Vaishnavism tradition, which emphasises the worship of Vishnu, the preserver of the universe. The text is divided into six books (amshas) and comprises approximately 23,000 verses.

The Purana provides a comprehensive narrative of the creation, preservation, and eventual dissolution of the universe, illustrating the cyclical nature of time in Hindu cosmology. The text begins with the story of creation, describing how Vishnu manifests as Brahma to create the universe and as Shiva to destroy it, thereby maintaining cosmic balance.

One of the most significant aspects of Vishnu Purana is its detailed recounting of the 10 avatars of Vishnu, including his famous incarnations as Rama and Krishna. Through these stories, the Purana highlights the role of Vishnu in protecting the world from evil forces and restoring dharma (righteousness).

In addition to mythology, the Purana offers insights into various aspects of Hindu philosophy, including the nature of the Self (atman), the importance of devotion (bhakti), and the principles of dharma. It also includes genealogies of gods, sages, and kings, tracing the lineages that connect divine beings with humanity.

Vishnu Purana is not only a theological and philosophical text but also a practical guide for living a righteous life. It discusses moral conduct, duties of individuals at different stages of life, and the importance of performing one's dharma.

Shiva Purana is dedicated primarily to the worship of Lord Shiva, the destroyer and transformer among the Hindu Trinity (trimurti), and is a crucial text for Shaivism, the sect that reveres Shiva as the supreme deity.

The text is divided into seven major sections (samhitas): Vidyeshvara, Rudra, Shata Rudra, Koti Rudra, Uma, Kailasa, and Vayaviya Samhitas. These sections cover a wide range of topics, including the creation of the universe, the stories of Shiva's various forms and manifestations, the significance of his consort Parvati, and their sons, Ganesha and Kartikeya.

Central to the Shiva Purana is the Rudra Samhita, which narrates the stories of Shiva's marriage to Parvati, the birth of Ganesha, and the exploits of Kartikeya. It also includes the famous Daksha yajna story, which explains the origin of

Shiva's fierce form as Virabhadra and the significance of the Shivalingam.

The Purana also delves into the concept of bhakti (devotion) towards Shiva, emphasising the importance of pure devotion, meditation, and worship of Shiva in the form of lingam. It outlines various rituals, festivals, and observances dedicated to Shiva, such as Mahashivaratri, and provides instructions on constructing temples and performing daily worship.

Philosophically, Shiva Purana explores the nature of the atman, the concept of karma, and the cyclical process of creation, preservation, and destruction. It presents Shiva as both transcendent and immanent, embodying the principles of destruction and regeneration essential to the universe's balance. The text also emphasises the unity of Shiva and Shakti (the divine feminine power), portraying them as the Ultimate Reality from which all creation emerges.

Vayu Purana is named after Vayu, the wind god and one of the Ashta-Dikpalas (guardians of the directions). The Purana is divided into four parts: Prakriya, Upodghata, Anushanga, and Upasamhara.

It begins with detailed descriptions of the creation of the universe, the cycles of time (yugas), and the genealogies of gods, sages, and kings. The text explains the cosmic order and the roles of various deities in maintaining it, particularly highlighting Vayu's importance as the life-giving force and his connection to the breath (prana) in all living beings.

One of the significant features of Vayu Purana is its detailed account of the geographical and cultural landscape of ancient India, including descriptions of rivers, mountains, and sacred places of pilgrimage. It also contains narratives about the solar and lunar dynasties, the origins of various sacred texts, and the duties of kings and subjects.

The Purana is particularly important for its discussion of Hindu rituals, festivals, and the concept of dharma (righteousness). It outlines the importance of performing one's duties according to their stage of life and social order, reflecting the Vedic traditions.

Philosophically, Vayu Purana delves into the nature of Self (atman), the concept of liberation (moksha), and the significance of devotion to Vishnu, Shiva, and other deities. It also includes esoteric teachings on yoga, meditation, and the role of a guru in spiritual practice, providing insights into the ancient wisdom that shaped the cultural and spiritual heritage of India.

Bhagavata Purana, also known as the Shrimad Bhagavatam, is one of the most revered of the Puranas, celebrated for its deep spiritual and devotional teachings. It is composed of 12 books (cantos), containing around 18,000 verses. It is particularly venerated in the Vaishnavism tradition, which emphasises the worship of Vishnu and his avatars.

The Purana is renowned for its emphasis on bhakti (devotion) as the supreme path to liberation. It recounts the stories of Lord Vishnu's various incarnations, with a special focus on the life and teachings of Lord Krishna, considered the most complete avatar of Vishnu. The tenth canto, which narrates Krishna's childhood and youth, including his playful exploits with the Gopis and his cosmic teachings in Bhagavad Gita, is particularly cherished by devotees.

The text not only details Krishna's divine pastimes but also offers profound philosophical insights, including discussions on the nature of Self, the universe, and the Ultimate Reality (Brahman). Through parables, stories, and dialogues, it presents complex metaphysical concepts in an accessible form, making it a spiritual guide for devotees across different ages.

Bhagavata Purana is also known for its narration of Rasa Lila, which explores the ecstatic dance of Krishna with the Gopis, symbolising the soul's intense love and longing for the divine. It inspires devotion, selfless love,. and the pursuit of a life dedicated to spiritual realisation. This Purana is one of the most widely read and recited texts in Hinduism, especially during festivals and religious gatherings.

Naradiya Purana is named after Sage Narada, known for his wisdom and devotion to Lord Vishnu. A key text in the Vaishnavism tradition, this Purana is particularly significant for its emphasis on bhakti of Lord Vishnu, reflecting the teachings and principles associated with Narada himself.

The Purana covers a wide range of topics, including the creation of the universe, the duties of different social classes, the significance of holy places, and the importance of performing rituals and ceremonies. It provides detailed instructions on the worship of Vishnu and other deities, outlining the benefits of reciting various hymns, mantras, and prayers.

One of the central themes of the Purana is the promotion of the chanting of the holy names of Vishnu as the most effective means of attaining liberation, particularly in the current age of Kali Yuga, characterised by moral decline and spiritual degradation. This emphasis on the power of nama-sankirtana (chanting the divine name) aligns with the teachings of the Bhakti movement, which spread throughout India during the medieval period.

The Purana also highlights the importance of pilgrimage to sacred sites, especially those associated with Vishnu, such as Mathura, Dwarka, and Badrinath. It extols the virtues of visiting these places and performing devotional acts, asserting that such practices lead to spiritual purification and divine grace.

In addition to its devotional aspects, Naradiya Purana offers guidance on various aspects of daily life, including ethical conduct, social duties, and the observance of religious festivals. It serves as a practical and spiritual guide for devotees, inspiring them to embrace the path of devotion and the transformative power of divine love.

Markandeya Purana is distinguished by its unique narrative style and specific focus on Sage Markandeya's experiences. Unlike other Puranas, this text does not strictly adhere to the typical Purana structure, which usually includes cosmology, genealogies, and temple lore. Instead, it offers a blend of mythology, philosophy, and stories that are interwoven with teachings on righteousness and devotion.

One of the most celebrated sections of this Purana is Devi Mahatmya, also known as Durga Saptashati or Chandi Path. It is a powerful hymn dedicated to Goddess Durga, depicting her as the supreme force of the universe. Devi Mahatmya presents three main episodes where the Goddess defeats demons Madhu and Kaitabha, Mahishasura, and Shumbha-Nishumbha, representing the victory of good over evil and the protection of dharma.

Another unique aspect of Markandeya Purana is its inclusion of discussions on human life stages, or the four Ashrama system of Brahmacharya, Grihastha, Vanaprastha, and Sannyasa. It also explores the concept of Pralaya, or cosmic dissolution, and offers a philosophical outlook on life, death, and rebirth, emphasising the impermanence of the material world. The Purana's narratives are rich in moral and ethical lessons, with stories that illustrate the consequences of actions, the importance of virtue, and the power of faith.

Unlike other Puranas, which often focus heavily on the worship of a particular deity, Markandeya Purana is more universal in its approach, promoting devotion to both Shiva and Vishnu, while also elevating the Goddess to the status of Ultimate Reality.

Agni Purana stands out among the Maha Puranas for its encyclopaedic content, attributed to fire-god Agni, who narrates it to Sage Vasishtha. This Purana is unique in its structure, offering a comprehensive guide to various subjects, including Vedic rituals, iconography, law, medicine, and warfare, rather than focusing solely on mythological stories.

One of the distinctive aspects of the Purana is its detailed instructions on temple construction and the crafting of idols, making it a valuable resource for architects and artisans. It outlines specific measurements and proportions for creating images of deities, providing a technical manual that has influenced Hindu temple architecture and iconography over centuries.

The Purana also delves into the art of warfare, offering insights into the training of soldiers, the organisation of armies, and the use of various weapons and strategies. This includes a detailed discussion on the science of archery (Dhanur Veda), which is rarely covered in other Puranas.

Additionally, Agni Purana is notable for its sections on Ayurveda, offering guidance on health, medicine, and the treatment of various diseases. It combines spiritual wisdom with practical knowledge, reflecting a holistic approach to life.

The text also includes summaries of the *Ramayana* and the *Mahabharata*, as well as discussions on philosophy, ethics, and the duties of different social classes, but it uniquely intertwines these with practical advice on daily life. Agni Purana is thus a distinctive text that serves as both a spiritual guide and a practical handbook, reflecting the diverse and integrated nature of Hindu knowledge and tradition.

Bhavishya Purana is known for its distinctive focus on prophecy and future events, as suggested by its name, which translates to 'The Purana of the Future'. Bhavishya Purana is divided into four parts or Parvas: Brahma, Madhyama, Pratisarga, and Uttara Parvas. Each section deals with different aspects of Hindu cosmology, mythology, and future predictions.

The Pratisarga Parva is particularly notable for its prophetic content, which includes predictions about the future dynasties, significant historical figures, and even the advent of different religious movements. It is unique among the Puranas because it ventures beyond the typical mythological and genealogical content, exploring the rise of empires, societal changes, and religious transformations that would occur in the future.

Bhavishya Purana also contains rituals, prayers, and instructions for various religious observances, such as celebration of festivals and worship of deities. It discusses the importance of maintaining dharma and the consequences of deviating from the path of virtue. While the prophetic nature of Bhavishya Purana has intrigued many, it also serves as a spiritual guide, providing insights into Hindu beliefs, practices, and the enduring battle between good and evil.

Brahmavaivarta Purana is revered for its detailed exposition of theology, cosmology, and devotional practices. The text is divided into four major parts or Khandas: Brahma, Prakriti, Ganapati, and Krishna Janma Khandas. Each part focuses on different aspects of the divine and the universe.

The Brahma Khanda elaborates on the creation of the universe, describing how the cosmos emerged from Brahma, the creator god. The Prakriti Khanda is devoted to the worship of the Goddess (Prakriti), particularly in her manifestations as Durga and Radha. It underscores the importance of the divine feminine, portraying the Goddess as the source of all creation and the ultimate power in the universe.

The Ganapati Khanda focuses on Ganesha, the elephant-headed god of wisdom and remover of obstacles. It narrates his origins, exploits, and the significance of his worship in Hindu rituals.

The Krishna Janma Khanda is the most celebrated section, dedicated to the life and times of Lord Krishna. It delves into his childhood, his playful interactions with the Gopis, his role as the divine lover of Radha, and his teachings on bhakti. This section also emphasises the significance of Radha-Krishna worship, presenting Radha as the supreme devotee and consort of Krishna, embodying pure love and devotion.

Brahmavaivarta Purana is particularly influential in the Gaudiya Vaishnavism tradition, where worship of Radha-Krishna is central. It serves as a rich source of insights into the nature of devotion and the deep connection between the divine and the devotee.

Linga Purana is focused specifically on the worship and significance of the Shivalingam, an abstract representation of Lord Shiva. Unlike other Puranas that cover a wide range of deities, Linga Purana is singularly dedicated to Shiva, offering profound insights into the symbolic and metaphysical meanings of the Linga.

One of the most distinctive features of the Purana is the story of the origin of the Linga itself. It is the story of the cosmic pillar of light, the Linga, which appeared when Brahma and Vishnu argued over who was superior. Shiva manifested as the infinite Linga to demonstrate the futility of their dispute, symbolising the formless, boundless nature of the divine.

The Purana also provides detailed instructions on the rituals and practices associated with Linga worship, emphasising on the importance of purity, devotion, and specific rites that should be performed during different times of the day and year. It outlines the construction of Shiva temples, the correct methods of Linga installation, and the benefits of various forms of worship, such as Abhisheka, the ritual bathing of the Linga.

Furthermore, the Purana delves into the esoteric aspects of the Linga, presenting it as a symbol of the union of Shiva and Shakti, the male and female principles that create and sustain the universe. It also discusses the Linga as a representation of the cosmic pillar, linking heaven, earth, and netherworld, and explores its significance in meditative and tantric practices.

Linga Purana is not merely a collection of myths but a deeply philosophical and ritualistic text that offers a comprehensive guide to the worship of Shiva through the Linga, making it a cornerstone for devotees and practitioners of Shaivism.

Varaha Purana is centred around the Varaha avatar of Lord Vishnu, where he incarnates as a boar to rescue the earth (personified as the Goddess Bhudevi) from the demon Hiranyaksha. Unlike other Puranas that spread their focus across multiple deities and themes, Varaha Purana is distinct for its deep exploration of this specific incarnation and its associated symbolism.

One of the key features of Varaha Purana is its vivid description of cosmology and geography from the perspective of the Varaha avatar. It provides a detailed account of the earth's creation and structure, as seen through the eyes of Vishnu in his boar form, offering insights into the ancient Hindu understanding of the universe. This text uniquely blends mythological narrative with cosmological theories, illustrating the earth's position within the broader cosmic order.

Varaha Purana is also significant for its detailed instructions on religious practices, particularly those related to the worship of Vishnu in his Varaha form. It discusses the importance of temples, pilgrimages, and specific rites associated with the Varaha avatar, such as the Varaha Jayanti, which celebrates the day Vishnu assumed this form.

Additionally, the Purana offers guidance on dharma, with particular emphasis on moral conduct, the duties of kings, and the ethical responsibilities of individuals across different stages of life. It also includes teachings on the benefits of various charitable acts, rituals, and observances, all framed within the context of devotion to Vishnu.

Skanda Purana is one of the largest and most intricate Puranas, focused on the exploits and significance of Skanda (also known as Kartikeya or Murugan), the god of war and son of Shiva and Parvati. Unlike other Puranas that cover multiple deities, the Skanda Purana dedicates itself primarily to Skanda's birth, his battles, and his role as the commander of the divine armies.

A distinctive aspect of Skanda Purana is its detailed recounting of Skanda's origins. It narrates how Skanda was born to destroy the demon Tarakasura, a menace to the gods. The Purana describes Skanda's extraordinary birth, and his subsequent upbringing by the Krittikas (the six Pleiades star cluster), which earned him the name Kartikeya.

Skanda Purana is also notable for its exhaustive pilgrimage guides, providing detailed descriptions of sacred sites across India, particularly those dedicated to Skanda. It outlines the significance of these places, the rituals to be performed, and the spiritual benefits of visiting them. Temples like those in Tamil Nadu, especially the six abodes of Murugan (Arupadai Veedu), are prominently featured.

Additionally, the Purana delves into the philosophical aspects of Shaivism, emphasising the importance of devotion to Shiva and Skanda. It also offers moral teachings through stories that illustrate the virtues of valour, righteousness, and devotion.

Vamana Purana is primarily focused on the Vamana avatar of Lord Vishnu, where he incarnates as a dwarf brahmin to restore cosmic order. This Purana explores Vamana's role in the cosmic struggle between the devas (gods) and asuras (demons), highlighting the balance between humility and power.

One of the central narratives of Vamana Purana is the story of King Bali, a righteous but ambitious asura who gains control over the three worlds through intense penance and devotion. The Purana details how Vishnu, in the form of Vamana, approaches Bali during a grand yajna and asks for three paces of land. In a remarkable twist, Vamana grows to encompass the universe, covering the earth and heaven in two steps and then placing his third step on Bali's head, symbolically granting Bali liberation while restoring cosmic order.

Beyond this core story, Vamana Purana provides elaborate descriptions of the universe's structure, geography, and the various realms of existence, as seen through the lens of this avatar. It also offers insights into the nature of dharma, emphasising themes of humility, sacrifice, and the proper use of power.

The Purana is also rich in its exploration of tirthas (sacred pilgrimage sites), particularly those associated with Vishnu in his Vamana form. It highlights the spiritual significance of these sites, offering guidance on the rituals and benefits associated with visiting them.

Kurma Purana is centred on the Kurma avatar of Lord Vishnu, where he incarnates as a tortoise to support Mount Mandara during the churning of the ocean, a pivotal event in Hindu cosmology. This Purana, unlike others, deeply intertwines the Kurma avatar with philosophical teachings, especially those related to Vaishnavism and Shaivism.

One of the standout features of Kurma Purana is its detailed narrative of the Samudra Manthan, or the churning of the ocean of milk, where gods and demons collaborated to extract the nectar of immortality (amrita). In this story, Vishnu, in his tortoise form, supports the mountain used as the churning rod, preventing it from sinking, thereby enabling the cosmic process. This avatar symbolises the support of the divine in maintaining the balance of the universe.

Beyond its mythological accounts, Kurma Purana is notable for its exposition on various forms of worship, including the significance of specific mantras and rituals dedicated to both Vishnu and Shiva. It uniquely bridges the worship practices of these two major godheads, reflecting the syncretic nature of Hindu worship.

The Purana also offers a rich discourse on ethical living, dharma, and the responsibilities of individuals across different life stages. It includes sections on yoga, meditation, and ascetic practices, presenting them as pathways to spiritual liberation.

Moreover, Kurma Purana is one of the few Puranas that provides detailed descriptions of various sacred rituals and observances, such as the Ekadashi fasts and their spiritual significance. It also elaborates on the merits of pilgrimage to holy sites, especially those associated with Vishnu's Kurma form.

Matsya Purana focuses on the Matsya avatar of Vishnu, where he takes the form of a great fish to save humanity and sacred knowledge from a catastrophic deluge. This Purana is unique in its combination of mythological narratives with detailed guidance on religious practices, temple architecture, and iconography.

The central narrative of Matsya Purana is the story of King Manu, the first human, who is warned by Matsya about an impending flood that would destroy the world. Vishnu, in his fish form, instructs Manu to gather the seeds of all living beings and the Veda into a boat. When the flood arrives, Matsya guides the boat to safety, ensuring the continuity of life and sacred knowledge. This tale reflects the themes of preservation and renewal.

Matsya Purana is also renowned for its detailed instructions on the construction of temples and crafting of idols. It provides specific measurements and proportions for creating images of deities, which have influenced Hindu temple architecture for centuries. This Purana is one of the few texts that offers such comprehensive guidance on religious art and architecture, making it invaluable for artists and builders.

Additionally, Matsya Purana covers a wide range of topics, including cosmology, genealogy, and duties of kings, but it uniquely intertwines these with practical advice on rituals, pilgrimage, and daily conduct, offering a holistic approach to living a righteous life.

Garuda Purana is notably distinct for its focus on eschatology, offering detailed descriptions of death, afterlife, and the rituals associated with funerals and ancestor worship. Unlike other Puranas, which often centre on cosmology or mythology, Garuda Purana provides a unique insight into the journey of the soul after death, making it one of the most significant texts for understanding Hindu concepts of mortality and rebirth.

A key aspect of Garuda Purana is its vivid depiction of the afterlife, where it outlines the journey of the soul through various realms, detailing the judgments passed based on one's karma. The Purana describes the various punishments in the hellish realms for sinful actions, as well as the rewards in heavenly realms for virtuous deeds. This section, known as the Pretakalpa, serves as a moral guide, emphasising the importance of living a righteous life to ensure a favourable rebirth.

The Purana also delves into the significance of performing Shraddha (ancestral rites) and the rituals for the deceased, offering specific instructions on how to conduct these ceremonies to aid the soul's passage to the afterlife. It is one of the primary sources detailing the procedures for these rites, which are widely followed in Hindu society.

Additionally, Garuda Purana covers topics like medicine, astrology, and gemmology, reflecting its encyclopaedic nature. However, it is its focus on the post-mortem journey and the ethical implications of one's actions that truly sets it apart from other Puranas.

The Garuda Purana is thus a critical text for understanding the Hindu worldview on life, death, and the afterlife, offering both philosophical insights and practical guidance on the rites and rituals that shape the human experience.

Brahmanda Purana is recognised for its comprehensive coverage of Hindu cosmology. The word *brahmanda* translates to 'The Cosmic Egg', symbolising the universe's origin and the broader cosmos, which is the central theme of this Purana.

Brahmanda Purana is notable for its detailed descriptions of the creation of the universe, including the cyclic process of creation, preservation, and dissolution (Srishti, Sthiti, and Laya). It narrates the genealogy of gods, sages, and kings, providing a rich tapestry of mythological stories that are integral to Hindu belief.

One of the Purana's key sections is the Lalita Sahasranama, a hymn that praises Goddess Lalita with a thousand names, emphasising the importance of Shakti worship in Hinduism.

This hymn is highly revered and is regularly recited by devotees to invoke the Goddess' blessings.

Brahmanda Purana also contains a wealth of information on astrology, rituals, offering guidance on religious observances and the significance of holy places. It discusses various pilgrimage sites, particularly in southern India, and the merits of visiting them. Additionally, the Purana includes predictions about future events, similar to the Bhavishya Purana, though in a more limited scope.

8
ITIHASA

Itihasa means 'it happened thus'. It is history as it truly happened. The objective of Itihasa and the Veda, however, is the same. Both try to convey the eternal truth. The only difference is that Itihasa explains the material and transcendental teachings of the Veda through interesting historical stories. They are meant for ordinary people who are unable to understand the Vedic philosophy as propounded in the four Vedas.

The two sacred texts classified as Itihasa in Hindu scriptures are the well-known epics, *Ramayana* and the *Mahabharata*. It is believed that they are responsible for keeping Hinduism alive.

RAMAYANA

Ramayana is a Sanskrit epic written by Sage Valmiki, revered as Adi Kavi or the first poet. Hence *Ramayana* is also known as Adi Kavya or the first epic. Valmiki composed the epic after being inspired by the divine tale of Lord Rama, which was revealed to him as Mula Ramayana by Sage Narada.

Valmiki created *Ramayana* to teach the principles of dharma (righteousness), karma (action), and the ideal conduct for individuals in various roles, such as a king, husband, wife, brother, and friend. Set in Treta Yuga, *Ramayana* narrates the story of Rama, the Lord Vishnu incarnate, a descendent of Ikshvaku clan belonging to the Solar Dynasty.

Throughout *Ramayana,* we find powerful arguments about what is right and what is wrong. These arguments are as relevant even today as they were at the time of Rama. The epic clearly points out that one's life should be in accordance with dharma, whether it results in pain or pleasure. It also stresses the importance of keeping up promises whatever may be the outcome.

Ramayana serves as a moral and spiritual guide, illustrating the ideal behaviours and relationships through its characters. Rama, the protagonist, embodies the ideals of dharma, selflessness, and duty, making him an exemplary figure for rulers and individuals alike. The epic also addresses the themes of good versus evil, the importance of family, and the consequences of actions driven by desire, greed, or pride.

Over the centuries, *Ramayana* has been adapted into numerous versions across different cultures and languages, each with its unique interpretations and emphasis. Some of the important adaptations include the 12th century Tamil *Ramavataram* and Kannada *Ramachandra Charitapurana,* 13th century Telugu *Sri Ranganatha Ramayanam,* and 17th century Malayalam *Adhyathmaramayanam Kilippattu.*

The 16th century *Awadhi Ramcharitmanas* by Goswami Tulsidas is a popular version of Valmiki's *Ramayana* that focuses on Rama's divine nature and is considered as the greatest book amongst all devotional literature.

Ramayana also spread to other Asian countries and the popular adaptations are the Cambodian *Reamker,* Indonesian *Kakawin Ramayana,* Thai *Ramakien,* Lao *Phra Lak Phra Ram* and Burmese *Yama Zatdaw.* Each version of *Ramayana* offers a unique perspective, yet all share the core narrative of Lord Rama's journey and the timeless teachings of the epic.

Ramayana has 24,000 verses spread over seven kands or books.

Bal Kand details the early life of Rama. It begins with the birth of Rama and his brothers, Bharata, Lakshman, and Shatrughna, to King Dasharatha of Ayodhya, after a long penance to have sons. The book narrates the early education and growth of the princes under Sage Vishwamitra. Rama's valour is showcased when he breaks the mighty bow of Lord Shiva, an act that wins him the hand of Sita, the daughter of King Janaka of Mithila, in marriage. Bal Kand sets the stage for Rama's future adventures, emphasising on his divine nature, righteousness, and the key relationships that will shape his journey. It also introduces significant characters like Ravana and Hanuman, whose roles become crucial later on in the story.

Ayodhya Kand focuses on the events leading up to Rama's exile. It begins with King Dasharatha's decision to crown Rama as his successor, a decision celebrated throughout Ayodhya. However, the joy is short-lived as Queen Kaikeyi, influenced by her attendant Manthara, demands the fulfilment of two boons previously granted by Dasharatha, which were, to exile Rama to the forest for 14 years and declare her son Bharata as the crown prince. Bound by his promise, Dasharatha reluctantly agrees, leading to a heart-wrenching farewell between Rama and his parents. Rama, along with his wife Sita and brother Lakshman, willingly embraces the exile, showcasing his adherence to dharma (righteousness). Ayodhya Kand highlights themes of duty, sacrifice, and the complexities of familial love, as well as the emotional turmoil of the royal family and the citizens of Ayodhya.

Aranya Kand chronicles the 13 years of Rama's exile in the forest, along with Sita and Lakshman. During this period, they visit many hermitages of sages, where Rama and Lakshman protect them from rakshasas (demons), deepening the spiritual and moral lessons of the epic. The story intensifies when demoness Surpanakha, infatuated with Rama, tries to harm Sita and is disfigured by Lakshman. Seeking revenge, Surpanakha instigates her brother Ravana, the powerful king of Lanka, to abduct Sita. With the help of demon Mareech, Ravana kidnaps Sita, leading to her sorrowful separation from Rama. Aranya Kand sets the stage for the epic's central conflict, highlighting the virtues of bravery, devotion, and the consequences of desire and vengeance.

Kishkindha Kand details Rama's quest to find Sita after her abduction by Ravana. Rama and Lakshman arrive in Kishkindha, the monkey kingdom, where they meet Hanuman, the devoted minister of the exiled monkey king Sugriva. Sugriva, having been dethroned by his brother Vali, seeks Rama's help to regain his kingdom. In return, Sugriva promises to assist Rama in finding Sita. Rama slays Vali, restoring Sugriva to power. True to his word, Sugriva assembles his monkey army to search for Sita. Hanuman's pivotal role begins in this Kand as he leaps across the ocean to Lanka, discovering Sita in Ravana's palace and assuring her that Rama will soon rescue her. Kishkindha Kand emphasises themes of friendship, loyalty, and the gathering of forces for the eventual battle against Ravana, setting the stage for the epic confrontation in Lanka.

Sundar Kand is the most revered Kand of the *Ramayana*, focusing on Hanuman's heroic journey to Lanka in search of Sita. It begins with Hanuman's mighty leap across the ocean, overcoming obstacles like demoness Surasa and mountain Mainaka. Upon reaching Lanka, Hanuman shrinks in size to avoid detection and explores the city, finally discovering Sita in the Ashoka Vatika, where she is held captive by Ravana. Hanuman approaches Sita, delivering Rama's message and assuring her of imminent rescue. To demonstrate his power and Rama's might, Hanuman allows himself to be captured by Ravana's forces, only to set Lanka ablaze with his burning tail before returning to Rama with news of Sita. Sundar Kand highlights Hanuman's unwavering devotion, courage, and resourcefulness, serving as a powerful reminder of the strength derived from faith, and the importance of selfless service in the face of adversity.

Yuddha Kand, also known as the Lanka Kand, is the most climactic book of the *Ramayana,* depicting the epic battle between Rama's forces and Ravana's army in Lanka. After receiving news of Sita's whereabouts from Hanuman, Rama, along with Lakshman, Sugriva, and their massive monkey army, builds a bridge across the ocean to reach Lanka. The war begins with fierce battles between the two sides, showcasing the valour and skills of warriors like Hanuman, Angada, and Ravana's son Indrajit. In a series of intense confrontations, Lakshman is grievously wounded, but is revived by the Sanjeevani herb brought by Hanuman. The climax arrives when Rama finally confronts Ravana in a monumental duel, ultimately slaying the demon king with a powerful arrow. Yuddha Kand concludes with Rama's reunion with Sita, the coronation of Vibhishana as the new king of Lanka, and Rama's triumphant return to Ayodhya, signifying the victory of good over evil.

Uttar Kand is an epilogue, dealing with the aftermath of the great war and the reign of Lord Rama in Ayodhya. It begins with Rama's return to Ayodhya, where he is crowned as king and establishes a just and prosperous rule. However, despite the victory over Ravana, the societal doubts regarding Sita's purity begin to surface. To uphold dharma and address public opinion, Rama, despite his personal anguish, decides to exile the pregnant Sita to the forest. In the forest, Sita takes refuge in the ashram of Sage Valmiki, where she gives birth to twin sons, Lava and Kusha. The boys grow up to be valiant and wise, eventually being recognised by Rama. Sita, in a final act of proving her purity, returns to the earth, her mother. Eventually Rama also departs to his heavenly abode, to reunite with Sita. Uttar Kand concludes the epic by reflecting on the complexities of duty, sacrifice, and the responsibilities of leadership.

There are some prominent Sanskrit versions of the *Ramayana* that focus on peripheral stories and philosophical expositions rather than the main narrative of Valmiki's story.

ADBHUTA RAMAYANA is a unique and lesser-known Sanskrit text attributed to Sage Valmiki, offering an unconventional retelling of the traditional *Ramayana* narrative in 27 Sargas (chapters). *Adbhuta* means 'wonderful' or 'extraordinary', reflecting the text's focus on miraculous and mystical events that differ significantly from those in the standard *Ramayana*. This *Ramayana* is considered part of the tantric and Shakta traditions within Hinduism and emphasises on the divine feminine power (Shakti) alongside the traditional focus on Lord Rama.

One of the most striking aspects of *Adbhuta Ramayana* is its portrayal of Sita, who is depicted not just as the devoted wife of Rama but as a powerful goddess in her own right. The text includes the story of the circumstances of Sita's birth and her fierce incarnation as Mahakali, who destroys the thousand-headed brother of Ravana. This narrative underscores the concept of Sita as an embodiment of the supreme Shakti, highlighting the strength and independence of the feminine divine.

Adbhuta Ramayana also includes additional stories and philosophical teachings that are not found in the traditional *Valmiki Ramayana*. It offers a more esoteric and symbolic interpretation of the epic, expanding its scope beyond the familiar narrative, making it valuable for understanding the broader spectrum of Hindu mythology and spirituality.

ADHYATMA RAMAYANA is a spiritual and philosophical retelling of *Ramayana* by Sage Vyasa. It is part of the larger Brahmanda Purana, and is considered as one of the most important works in the Advaita Vedanta tradition. The text emphasises the non-dualistic (advaita) interpretation of the epic, where Lord Rama is portrayed not just as a human prince but as the Supreme Being, an incarnation of Lord Vishnu.

This version of *Ramayana* is concise, consisting of about 4,500 verses divided into seven Kandas (books), similar to the original *Ramayana*. However, it places a strong emphasis on the spiritual teachings and divine nature of Rama, unlike Valmiki's version that emphasises on his human nature. The narrative intertwines Rama's story with deep philosophical discussions, particularly focusing on the nature of the Self (atman), the illusory nature of the world (maya), and the path to liberation (moksha).

A key aspect of *Adhyatma Ramayana* is its portrayal of the relationship between Rama and Sita. Sita is depicted as the embodiment of pure consciousness (chitta), and her separation from Rama symbolises the individual soul's separation from the Supreme Consciousness. The text also introduces the famous 'Rama Nama' mantra, highlighting the power of chanting Rama's name for spiritual liberation.

This *Ramayana* is revered for its ability to blend devotional elements with profound spiritual wisdom, making it a cherished text for those seeking both bhakti (devotion) and jnana (knowledge). Goswami Tulsidas' *Ramcharitmanas* is believed to be inspired by it.

ANANDA RAMAYANA is a lesser-known yet significant Sanskrit text that offers an alternate retelling of *Ramayana*.

Ananda means 'bliss', reflecting the joy and devotion it inspires in its readers. This version is attributed to Sage Valmiki, though it is distinct from the original *Ramayana* in its emphasis on the divine and miraculous aspects of Lord Rama's life.

Ananda Ramayana is divided into seven Kandas (books), much like the traditional *Ramayana,* but it includes additional narratives and embellishments not found in the other version. One of its most notable features is the elaborate descriptions of the rituals and celebrations surrounding Rama's birth and coronation. It also delves into events that occur after the main story, such as the return of Lord Rama to his divine abode, Vaikuntha, and the worship of Rama by various gods and sages.

The text places a strong emphasis on the devotional aspects of Rama's character, highlighting his divine nature and the joy experienced by his devotees. It also includes the Rama Raksha Stotra, a powerful hymn for protection.

Ananda Ramayana is cherished in certain devotional traditions, where it serves as a source of inspiration and spiritual guidance, offering a more devotional and celebratory perspective on Lord Rama's life.

YOGA VASISTHA is a profound philosophical text attributed to Sage Valmiki. Unlike the original *Ramayana,* Yoga Vasistha delves deeply into the nature of reality, consciousness, and liberation, making it a key text in Advaita Vedanta and other non-dualistic schools of Hindu philosophy.

The text is structured as a dialogue where young Rama, troubled by the existential questions of life, seeks guidance from his spiritual teacher, Vasistha. Vasistha responds by recounting various stories, parables, and discourses that explore the nature of Self, the illusory nature of the world (maya), and the path to spiritual liberation (moksha). The central theme is that the world is a projection of the mind, and by understanding this, one can transcend the cycle of birth and death.

Yoga Vasistha is divided into six sections: Vairagya-prakaranam (dispassion), Mumukshuvayahara-prakaranam (seeking), Utpatti-prakaranam (creation), Sthiti-prakaranam (existence), Upashama-prakaranam (tranquillity), and Nirvana-prakaranam (liberation). The text is highly regarded for its intellectual depth, metaphysical insights, and emphasis on self-inquiry.

Yoga Vasistha is more of a spiritual treatise than a historical epic, focusing on inner exploration and the ultimate truth rather than external events, making it a valuable resource for those on the spiritual path.

MAHABHARATA

The *Mahabharata* is one of the most important and extensive epics in world literature, written by Sage Vyasa. It is a monumental work consisting of over 100,000 shlokas (verses) across 18 parvas (books), making it the longest epic poem ever written.

The *Mahabharata* narrates the complex and multi-layered story of the Kuru dynasty of the Lunar race, focusing on the conflict between two branches of the family, the Pandavas and the Kauravas, culminating in the epic Kurukshetra War. It is based in Dwapar Yuga. The epic is not linear, it has many ancient myths and legends interwoven into the main story. It does not revolve around any one central figure but has many heroic characters, among which, Lord Vishnu's incarnation Krishna is of primary importance.

Through this story, Vyasa imparts profound moral, philosophical, and spiritual lessons to humanity. The epic addresses the complexities of human life, exploring themes like dharma (righteousness), karma (action and consequence), justice, loyalty, and the struggle between good and evil. The purpose of the *Mahabharata* is not only to tell the story of a great war but to serve as a guide to righteous living and the understanding of life's challenges.

One of the most significant sections of the *Mahabharata* is Bhagavad Gita, a 700-verse dialogue between Prince Arjuna and Lord Krishna, which provides a comprehensive guide to living a life of virtue, duty, and devotion.

The *Mahabharata's* vast narrative serves as a mirror to human nature, illustrating the eternal conflict between moral duty and personal desire. The epic's deep philosophical insights make it an essential text in Hindu tradition, offering guidance on how to live a life of meaning and integrity amidst the complexities of the world.

The *Mahabharata* has been adapted, translated, and retold in numerous versions across different cultures and languages, much like the *Ramayana*.

Tamil *Mahabharata*, known as the *Villibharatham*, was written by the poet Villiputturar.

Nannaya, Tikkana, and Errana translated and adapted the epic into Telugu, creating a highly respected Telugu *Mahabharata* in the Andhra region. Several Malayalam adaptations exist, including the *Bharatha Paryatanam* by Ramapurathu Warrier. Kumara Vyasa's *Karnata Bharata Kathamanjari* is a celebrated Kannada version. Kashiram Das created a popular Bengali retelling of the epic as Bengali *Mahabharata*. The Marathi *Mahabharata*, known as Pandu Ranga's adaptation, is also significant.

The Indonesian shadow puppet theatre tradition has its own version of the *Mahabharata*, *Wayang Kulit*, adapted to fit local cultural contexts. The *Mahabharata* has also been adapted into various forms in Thailand and Java, often focusing on specific characters like Bhima or Arjuna.

These versions of the *Mahabharata* vary in content, emphasis, and interpretation, reflecting the cultural, religious, and philosophical contexts in which they were created. The epic's adaptability has allowed it to remain relevant across different times and places, making it an important part of global literature.

The *Mahabharata* has 18 parvas or books.

Adi Parva (The Book of the Beginning) serves as the foundation of the *Mahabharata*, detailing the origins and genealogies of the key characters and families central to the epic. It begins with the story of how the *Mahabharata* was composed by Vyasa and dictated to Ganesha. This parva traces the lineage of the Kuru dynasty, introducing characters like Bhishma, Dhritarashtra, Pandu, and Vidura. It narrates the birth and early life of the Pandavas and Kauravas, their education under Drona, and the development of their rivalry. Significant stories include the tale of Shakuntala, the story of Devavrata's vow (which earned him the name Bhishma), and the account of how the Pandavas came to marry Draupadi. Adi Parva sets the stage for the epic conflict by establishing the complex relationships, moral dilemmas, and the seeds of enmity that will later culminate in the Kurukshetra War.

Sabha Parva (The Book of the Assembly Hall) centres around the events in the grand assembly hall built by the Pandavas at Indraprastha, symbolising their rise to power. Yudhishthira performs the Rajasuya Yajna, a royal consecration ritual, which establishes him as an emperor. The parva's most significant event is the game of dice, masterminded by Duryodhana and Shakuni, in which Yudhishthira loses everything, including his kingdom, brothers, and Draupadi. The humiliation of Draupadi in the Kaurava court becomes a pivotal moment, setting the tone for the inevitable war. Despite Draupadi's plea for justice and the intervention of divine forces, the Pandavas are forced into exile for twelve years, followed by a year of incognito existence. Sabha Parva is crucial as it highlights the moral and ethical degradation in the Kaurava court, foreshadowing the impending conflict.

Aranyaka Parva or Vana Parva (The Book of the Forest) chronicles the 12 years of exile that the Pandavas spend in the forest after losing in the game of dice. The parva explores the hardships and trials they endure, focusing on their moral and spiritual growth during this period. The Pandavas encounter various sages, deities, and mythical creatures, each imparting wisdom and guidance. Notable stories within this parva include the tale of Nala and Damayanti, the teachings of Sage Markandeya, and Arjuna's quest to acquire celestial weapons from the gods. The parva also delves into the internal struggles of the characters, particularly Yudhishthira's reflections on dharma and justice. Aranyaka Parva serves as a period of preparation for the Pandavas, both mentally and physically, as they ready themselves for the challenges that lie ahead in their quest to reclaim their kingdom.

Virata Parva (The Book of Virata) recounts the thirteenth year of the Pandavas' exile, during which they live incognito in the kingdom of King Virata. To remain undetected, each Pandava, as well as Draupadi, assume different disguises and take up various roles in the king's court. The Kauravas, suspecting the presence of the Pandavas in Virata's kingdom, attempt to unmask them. A key event is the battle in which

Arjuna, disguised as a eunuch named Brihannala, reveals his true identity by single-handedly defeating the Kauravas and rescuing Virata's kingdom. This parva ends with the successful completion of the Pandavas' year of incognito exile, allowing them to reclaim their true identities and prepare for their return to Hastinapur. Virata Parva is significant as it marks the end of the Pandavas' period of suffering and their transition back into the political arena.

Udyoga Parva (The Book of Effort) focuses on the diplomatic efforts and preparations for war between the Pandavas and Kauravas. Following the end of their exile, the Pandavas demand the return of their kingdom, but Duryodhana refuses to cede even a small portion of the land. Various attempts are made to avoid conflict, including Krishna's peace mission to Hastinapur, where he tries to mediate a settlement. However, Duryodhana's stubbornness and the refusal of the Kauravas to compromise make war inevitable. The parva also includes important discussions on dharma and the duties of kings, as well as the gathering of allies and the formation of strategies by both sides. Udyoga Parva culminates in the final preparations for the Kurukshetra War, with both armies assembling on the battlefield. This parva highlights the tragic inevitability of war when diplomacy fails and sets the stage for the epic confrontation that follows.

Bhishma Parva (The Book of Bhishma) covers the first 10 days of the Kurukshetra War, during which Bhishma, the grandsire of both the Pandavas and Kauravas, leads the Kaurava army. This parva is particularly significant as it contains Bhagavad Gita, the sacred discourse given by Krishna to Arjuna on the battlefield, addressing Arjuna's moral dilemma about fighting the war. The parva details the strategies, formations, and battles that take place during this period, with Bhishma proving to be an almost invincible commander. However, despite his valour, Bhishma's deep love for both sides prevents him from fighting with full force against the Pandavas. The parva concludes with Bhishma's fall on the battlefield, struck down by Arjuna with the help of Shikhandi, who is born to be Bhishma's nemesis. Bhishma's fall marks a turning point in the war, symbolising the beginning of the end for the Kauravas.

Drona Parva (The Book of Drona) describes the phase of the Kurukshetra War when Drona, the revered teacher of both the Pandavas and Kauravas, takes command of the Kaurava army after Bhishma's fall. Drona proves to be a formidable leader, employing various military strategies and formations, including the Chakravyuha, which leads to the death of Abhimanyu, Arjuna's young and valiant son. This parva is marked by intense and ruthless fighting, with heavy casualties on both sides. The parva explores themes of duty, loyalty, and the tragic consequences of war. Drona's own death comes as a result of a deceptive tactic by the Pandavas, where he is led to believe that his son Ashwatthama is dead. Grief-stricken, Drona lays down his arms and is killed by Drishtadyumna. Drona Parva highlights the moral complexities of war and the devastating impact of losing loved ones in battle.

Karna Parva (The Book of Karna) centres on the period of the Kurukshetra War when Karna takes command of the Kaurava army after Drona's death. This parva is crucial as it explores the character of Karna, his loyalty to Duryodhana, and his tragic fate. Despite being one of the greatest warriors on the battlefield, Karna faces numerous challenges, which lead to his vulnerability. The parva is marked by Karna's final, fateful encounter with Arjuna, where he is ultimately killed. Karna Parva delves into themes of fate, identity, and the consequences of past actions. Karna's death marks the unravelling of Duryodhana's hopes and is a significant turning point in the war, as the Kaurava forces begin to collapse. The parva is a poignant exploration of Karna's internal struggles, his sense of duty, and the tragedy of his life.

Shalya Parva (The Book of Shalya) narrates the events of the final days of the Kurukshetra War, with Shalya, the king of Madra, reluctantly leading the Kaurava army after Karna's death. Shalya, though a skilled warrior, is not fully committed to the Kaurava cause, leading to demoralisation among the troops. The parva is marked by the intense and brutal final battle between the remaining forces. Bhima's mace duel with Duryodhana is one of the most significant events in this parva, where Bhima fulfils his vow to break Duryodhana's thigh, leading to the latter's defeat and the fall of the Kaurava empire. The Shalya Parva reflects on the futility of the war, the loss of life, and the destruction of the Kuru dynasty. The parva concludes with Duryodhana's death, signalling the end of war and the victory of Pandavas, albeit at a great cost.

Sauptika Parva (The Book of the Sleeping Warriors) describes the grim events that unfold on the night after the Kurukshetra War has effectively ended. Ashwatthama, the son of Drona, seeking revenge for his father's death, attacks the Pandava camp under the cover of darkness. Along with Kritavarma and Kripacharya, he massacres the sleeping warriors, including the five sons of Draupadi, who are mistakenly believed to be the Pandavas. The parva depicts the horrifying and unethical nature of this act, highlighting the theme of vengeance and its destructive consequences. Sauptika Parva serves as a sombre reflection on the aftermath of war, showing that even after victory, the wounds of conflict continue to fester, leaving behind a legacy of grief and bitterness.

Stree Parva (The Book of the Women) is a deeply emotional section of the *Mahabharata* that deals with the aftermath of the Kurukshetra War, focusing on the grief and mourning of the women who have lost their husbands, sons, and fathers in the conflict. The parva portrays the heart-wrenching scenes of the widows and mothers of the fallen warriors as they visit the battlefield, lamenting the loss of their loved ones. The parva also highlights the futility of war and the devastating consequences it brings to families and society. Queen Gandhari, the mother of the Kauravas, curses Krishna for allowing the destruction of the Kuru dynasty, leading to the eventual demise of his own Yadava clan. This parva serves as a powerful reminder of the tragic cost of war and the suffering it inflicts on those left behind.

Shanti Parva (The Book of Peace) is one of the longest and most philosophical sections of the *Mahabharata*. It is divided into three sub-parvas: the Rajadharma (duties of kings), Apaddharma (duties in times of distress), and Mokshadharma (duties related to liberation). After the war, Yudhishthira is crowned as the king of Hastinapur, but he is deeply troubled by the destruction caused by the conflict. Bhishma, lying on his deathbed of arrows, instructs Yudhishthira on the principles of dharma, governance, and righteousness. He imparts valuable lessons on how to rule justly, handle crises, and pursue spiritual enlightenment. The parva emphasises the importance of ethical leadership, the duties of a king, and the path to achieving peace and liberation. Bhishma's discourse in the Shanti Parva is considered as one of the most important treatises on morality and governance in Hindu philosophy.

Anushasana Parva (The Book of Instructions) continues the teachings of Bhishma to Yudhishthira, focusing on various aspects of dharma and the duties of individuals in different stages of life. Bhishma elaborates on the conduct of kings, the importance of charity, the roles of women, and the rules of dharma. He also discusses the duties of different varnas (castes) and ashramas (stages of life), providing guidance on how to lead a righteous and fulfilling life. The parva includes discussions on topics such as truth, non-violence, and the responsibilities of rulers towards their subjects. Bhishma's teachings in this parva are comprehensive, covering both worldly and spiritual aspects of life, and are intended to help Yudhishthira rule his kingdom wisely and justly. The parva concludes with Bhishma's death, marking the end of his long and revered life.

Ashvamedhika Parva (The Book of the Horse Sacrifice) describes the Ashvamedha Yajna (horse sacrifice) performed by Yudhishthira as part of his duty as a king to assert his sovereignty and seek the blessings of gods. The parva begins with Krishna encouraging Yudhishthira to perform the yajna to cleanse the sins of the war and to establish his rule over the land. A sacrificial horse is let loose to roam freely, and the territories it covers are challenged by Arjuna, who leads the army to subdue any opposition. The parva narrates the adventures and battles Arjuna faces during the campaign, including encounters with various kings. The yajna concludes successfully, symbolising the restoration of order and prosperity in the kingdom. The parva also includes the story of reunion of Arjuna with his son Babhruvahana.

Ashramavasika Parva (The Book of the Hermitage) deals with the final years of the elders of the Kuru dynasty, particularly Dhritarashtra, Gandhari, and Kunti, who retire to the forest to spend their last days in austerity and penance. The parva explores the themes of renunciation, detachment, and the inevitability of death. Yudhishthira, now ruling the kingdom, frequently visits them in the forest, providing them with support and care. The parva poignantly describes the deep sense of loss and sorrow experienced by these elders as they come to terms with the destruction of their family. Eventually, Dhritarashtra, Gandhari, and Kunti die in a forest fire, symbolising the end of the old generation. The parva reflects on the transient nature of life and the importance of letting go of worldly attachments, preparing for the final journey towards liberation.

Mausala Parva (The Book of the Clubs) narrates the tragic end of the Yadava dynasty, the clan of Krishna, through a curse that leads to their self-destruction. The parva begins with a curse placed on the Yadavas by sages, which results in the members of the clan engaging in a violent brawl, ultimately leading to their annihilation using clubs (mausala) made from iron. The parva describes the downfall of the once-glorious Yadava dynasty, marking the beginning of the end for the epic's divine and heroic era. Krishna, realising that the time has come for his departure from the earthly realm, withdraws to the forest, where he is accidentally killed by a hunter named Jara, who mistakes him for a deer. The parva highlights the themes of fate, destiny, and the cyclical nature of time, showing that even the mightiest must eventually face their end.

Mahaprasthanika Parva (The Book of the Great Journey) recounts the final journey of the Pandavas and Draupadi as they renounce their kingdom and worldly life to ascend to the heavens. After ruling the kingdom for many years, Yudhishthira decides to undertake the Mahaprasthana (great departure) along with his brothers and Draupadi. They set out on a journey towards the Himalayas, symbolising their gradual detachment from the material world. Along the way, the Pandavas and Draupadi, one by one, fall and die due to their human flaws, leaving only Yudhishthira to complete the journey. A dog, representing dharma, accompanies Yudhishthira throughout the journey. The parva explores the themes of renunciation, the consequences of one's actions, and the ultimate truth that all must face death.

Swargarohana Parva (The Book of the Ascension to Heaven) is the final book of the *Mahabharata*, describing Yudhishthira's ascent to heaven and the resolution of the epic's moral and spiritual questions. Yudhishthira, accompanied by the dog (dharma), reaches the gates of heaven, where he is tested by the gods. He initially refuses to enter heaven without his brothers and Draupadi, but is eventually reunited with them after enduring a final test of his righteousness. The parva reveals that the Pandavas and Kauravas, despite their earthly enmity, are ultimately granted a place in heaven, symbolising the idea that all souls are purified and reconciled in the afterlife. The parva brings the epic to a close with the triumph of dharma and the eternal reunion of the souls in the divine realm.

HARI VAMSHA (An appendix to the *Mahabharata*)

Hari Vamsha is a significant supplement to the *Mahabharata*. Attributed to Sage Vyasa, the author of the *Mahabharata*, Hari Vamsha serves to expand upon the life and deeds of Lord Krishna, providing a more comprehensive account that the main epic only touches upon briefly.

According to traditional accounts, Hari Vamsha was first recited by the great Sage Vaishampayana to King Janamejaya, the son of Parikshit. During this initial recital, Ugrashrava, also known as Suta, was present in the assembly. Later, at the request of the sages led by Sage Shaunaka at Naimisaranya, Suta narrated Hari Vamsha to them. This sequence of narration highlights the oral tradition through which ancient texts were preserved and transmitted across generations.

Composed of more than 16,000 verses, Hari Vamsha is divided into three parts. The first one is Harivamsha Parva, which elaborates on Krishna's ancestry, tracing his roots to the Yadava dynasty and detailing the cosmic origins of his family. The second part is Vishnu Parva that narrates Krishna's birth, his playful childhood, and his role as a divine protector, emphasising his avatars and miraculous deeds. The last part is Bhavishya Parva, which contains prophecies and discusses future events, offering a cosmic perspective on Vishnu's role in the universe.

Hari Vamsha bridges the *Mahabharata* with the later Puranas, particularly Vishnu Purana and Bhagavata Purana. It is revered for its theological insights and its portrayal of Krishna as both a supreme deity and a beloved figure in Hindu tradition.

BHAGAVAD GITA (The Song of God)

Bhagavad Gita, often referred to simply as Gita, is a 700-verse scripture that is an important part of the *Mahabharata*. Set within the Bhishma Parva of the epic, Gita is presented as a dialogue between Prince Arjuna and Lord Krishna, who serves as his charioteer. This conversation takes place on the battlefield of Kurukshetra, just before the start of the great war between the cousins Pandavas and Kauravas.

Though written by Sage Vyasa, Bhagavad Gita was narrated by his disciple, Sage Vaishampayana to King Janamejaya, as part of the larger narration of the *Mahabharata* itself. Within the epic, the actual conversation between Krishna and Arjuna was first heard by Sanjaya, who was granted divine vision by Sage Vyasa to witness the events of the battlefield and relay them to the blind Kaurava King Dhritarashtra.

Bhagavad Gita is a profound spiritual and philosophical discourse, exploring complex themes such as duty, righteousness, and the nature of reality. Arjuna, faced with the moral dilemma of fighting against his own relatives, friends and teachers, is gripped by doubt and despair. In response, Krishna imparts to him wisdom that transcends the immediate context of war, addressing the eternal struggles of the human soul.

Gita's teachings are universal, offering guidance on how to live a life of righteousness and balance. Krishna explains the concepts of karma (action), bhakti (devotion), and jnana (knowledge), while also revealing his divine nature. One of the key messages of Gita is the importance of performing one's duty without attachment to the results, a philosophy known as Nishkama Karma. Through his dialogue, Krishna also introduces the idea of eternal soul (atman), the transient nature of the physical body, and the ultimate goal of achieving union with the Divine.

Bhagavad Gita's impact has been profound and far-reaching. Countless scholars, spiritual leaders and even scientists across the globe have interpreted and commented upon its timeless wisdom over the centuries. Gita's teachings on the paths of devotion, action, and knowledge offer a comprehensive approach to achieving spiritual liberation and understanding one's place in the cosmos.

Till date, Bhagavad Gita remains the most influential scripture across various spiritual traditions worldwide.

However, other texts named 'Gita' exist as well.

ANU GITA was narrated by Krishna to Arjuna after the Kurukshetra war when the Pandavas established their kingdom. This text revisits key philosophical teachings, emphasising the nature of Self and the path to liberation.

ASHTAVAKRA GITA is a discourse by Sage Ashtavakra to King Janaka, which delves into the essence of Self and the illusory nature of the material world, emphasising on liberation.

AVADHUTA GITA is a poetic expression of spiritual freedom by Dattatreya. The text celebrates the state of an enlightened being who transcends dualities and lives in a state of pure awareness.

GANESH GITA is a dialogue between Lord Ganesha and King Varenya. The teachings show the path to liberation through righteousness and understanding of Self.

GURU GITA, part of Skanda Purana, is a dialogue where Lord Shiva teaches his wife Parvati about the significance of a Guru (spiritual teacher) in guiding the disciple towards liberation.

MOKSHA GITA is a concise text that outlines the path to moksha (liberation), providing practical teachings on how to overcome ignorance and realise the ultimate truth of Self.

RIBHU GITA is a dialogue between Lord Shiva and Sage Ribhu, focusing on the non-dualistic nature of reality and the realisation of Self as Brahman, the ultimate truth.

UDDHAVA GITA is a conversation between Krishna and his devotee Uddhava, where Krishna imparts teachings on detachment, devotion, and the impermanence of life, as he prepares to leave the mortal world.

VYADHA GITA is a discourse by a humble butcher who teaches a yogi the importance of duty, patience, and wisdom, revealing profound spiritual truths in the context of everyday life.

9

VEDANGA

The Vedanga are the explanatory limbs or *anga* of the Veda. They developed towards the end of the Vedic period, because the language of the Vedas seemed too archaic to the people of that time. There are six Vedanga or aspects of Vedic knowledge: Shiksha, Chhanda, Vyakarana, Nirukta, Kalpa and Jyotisha. Each Vedanga focuses on a specific aspect of Vedic knowledge, ensuring the accurate preservation, recitation, and application of the Veda.

Shiksha focuses on the phonetics and phonology of Sanskrit. Its primary aim is to ensure the correct pronunciation and intonation of Vedic texts, as precise pronunciation is crucial for preserving the sanctity and meaning of the hymns. Shiksha covers various aspects such as Swara (intonation), Varna (letters), Matra (quantity of sound), Balam (stress), Sama (evenness), and Santana (continuity). By mastering these elements, practitioners maintain the oral tradition and prevent corruption of the sacred Vedic chants.

Chhanda is the study of Vedic metre and prosody. It provides rules and guidelines for the arrangement of syllables and words in poetic verses, ensuring rhythm, structure, and harmony in Vedic chanting. Chhanda is essential for maintaining the musicality and aesthetic quality of the Vedic texts, as well as for preserving their intended meaning and pronunciation. Various metres, such as Gayatri, Anushtubh, Trishtubh, and Jagati, dictate the number of syllables and the arrangement of long and short syllables, allowing precise and consistent Vedic recitation.

Vyakarana focuses on the study of Sanskrit grammar. It serves as an essential tool for understanding and interpreting the Vedic texts accurately and preserving their integrity. The most notable work in this field is Panini's Ashtadhyayi, a detailed treatise written around the 4th century BCE. Panini's work systematically outlines the phonetics, morphology, and syntax of Sanskrit, setting a foundation for future linguistic studies.

Nirukta is the study of the etymology and explanation of difficult words in the Vedic texts. It provides a systematic approach to understanding the meaning and context of Vedic hymns and mantras by explaining the roots, formation, and usage of words. Compiled by Yaska, the Nirukta text offers commentaries and interpretations of obscure or ambiguous terms. This Vedanga is crucial for preserving the accuracy and clarity of Vedic knowledge, ensuring that the scriptures are comprehensible and meaningful to future generations of scholars and practitioners. Nirukta is the basis for the later lexicons and dictionaries.

Kalpa deals with the procedural and ritualistic aspects of Vedic ceremonies. It encompasses the guidelines and instructions for conducting various rituals, sacrifices (yajnas), and daily religious practices. Kalpa includes several sub-disciplines like Shrauta Sutras (rituals described in the Vedas), Grihya Sutras (domestic rituals), Dharma Sutras (social and legal norms), and Shulba Sutras (rules for constructing sacrificial altars). These texts provide detailed instructions on performing ceremonies accurately and effectively. The primary aim of Kalpa is to ensure that Vedic rituals are conducted in a prescribed and standardised manner, maintaining the sanctity and efficacy of these sacred practices.

Jyotisha is the study of astronomy and astrology, designed to determine the auspicious timing for Vedic rituals and sacrifices. It involves observation of celestial bodies, such as the sun, moon, and planets, to guide the timing of religious ceremonies and daily activities. Jyotisha includes mathematical calculations and predictions about celestial events, helping practitioners align their practices with cosmic rhythms. This Vedanga ensures that rituals are performed at times believed to be cosmically harmonious and spiritually beneficial.

The Vedanga maintain the integrity and continuity of the Vedic tradition, bridging the gap between ancient and contemporary understanding, thus forming a strong foundation for traditional Hindu education.

10
UPA VEDA

Upa Veda are supplementary texts of the Veda. There are four Upa Veda, each associated with a specific main Veda and dedicated to practical aspects of life. Sthapatya Veda (tied to Rig Veda), focuses on architecture and craftsmanship. Gandharva Veda (related to Sama Veda), covers music, dance, and aesthetics. Dhanur Veda (linked to Yajur Veda), details martial arts and warfare. Ayurveda (connected to Atharva Veda), focuses on medicine and health. These texts enhance the spiritual teachings of the Veda by applying them to daily life and various fields of knowledge.

Sthapatya Veda is the traditional Indian science of architecture and construction that is considered a branch of the Rig Veda. It focuses on principles of design, layout, measurements, ground preparation, space arrangement, and spatial geometry. Central to the text is the concept of harmony with nature and the cosmic forces, emphasising the balance between structure, environment, and the individuals living within it. It aims to create buildings that promote health, prosperity, and spiritual well-being, by adhering to the rules of orientation, proportions, and aesthetics outlined in the Rig Veda.

Gandharva Veda, considered a branch of Sama Veda, is the Vedic science of music and performing arts. It encompasses the study of sound, melody, and rhythm, detailing the principles and techniques of Indian classical music, dance, and other art forms. The Veda is rooted in the concept of Nada Brahma, meaning 'sound is divine'. It explores how music influences the mind and consciousness, with a focus on creating spiritual upliftment.

Dhanur Veda, a supplement to Yajur Veda, is the ancient Indian science of warfare and martial arts. It contains both offensive and defensive techniques of warfare, including training in archery, swordsmanship, and other weapons, as well as strategies for combat and military organisation. The Veda details the physical, mental, and spiritual preparation necessary for warriors, emphasising on ethics, discipline, and skill. The teachings extend beyond the battlefield, focusing on the warrior's role in upholding dharma and protecting society. It combines ritualistic practices with practical guidance, aiming to cultivate a balanced and righteous warrior dedicated to the greater good.

Ayurveda, rooted in Atharva Veda, is an ancient Indian system of medicine and holistic healing. It emphasises the balance of the body, mind, and spirit to achieve overall health and well-being. Ayurveda is based on the five elements: earth, water, fire, air, and ether, and the three doshas: Vata, Pitta, and Kapha, that influence individual constitution and health. It encompasses various practices, including herbal medicine, diet, yoga, meditation, and bodywork. The primary goal of Ayurveda is to prevent illness, promote longevity, and maintain harmony by aligning the individual's lifestyle with nature's rhythms and laws.

11

DARSHANA

Darshana means seeing or envisioning, in this case, the Truth. The ancient sages explained the inherent philosophy of Veda in different ways according to their vision, called Darshana. There are six ways of perceiving the Ultimate Truth and hence, Shad Darshana or six Darshanas. But unlike the Veda and Upanishad, they are not regarded as revelations.

The Darshana are based on reason and logic, even though they accept the primacy of the Veda. The sages used reason and axioms to establish their philosophies and address the fundamental issues of the basis of existence, reality, the nature of matter, life and spirit, the destiny of the individual, the existence and nature of soul, and so on.

The six Darshanas are Nyaya, Vaisheshika, Sankhya, Yoga, Purva Mimamsa and Uttara Mimamsa.

Nyaya Darshana (Logical School) was founded by Sage Gautama in 4th century BC. It is based on logic and realism, accepting what we see and what we experience through our senses. It says that the test of the Truth is whether it can be repeated and practised, and whether it leads to useful action. Basically, Truth is known through its utility.

Nyaya is a science of debate and discussions, hence also called Tarka Shastra. It has an elaborate system of logic and 16 categories of the techniques of reasoning, including doubting, arguing constructively or destructively, attacking vulnerable points of the opponent's argument, using established facts, and so on.

Nyaya seeks to prove the existence of God using logic. It says that the universe must have come from somewhere, that there exists order in the universe, and that no one has ever proved that God does not exist. It also says that there are many souls, each going through cycles of birth and death according to its karma. A soul is released from this cycle when it gains knowledge. Nyaya defines the release or liberation as absence of pain, and not as bliss.

Vaisheshika Darshana (Atomic School) was propounded by Sage Kanada around 6th century BC. It says that the source of all knowledge is perception and logic. According to this system, the cause of cosmic manifestation is nothing but a combination of atoms in different ways. It holds that the smallest, indivisible and indestructible unit of the universe is the atom. It uses logic to establish this premise. The atom is made active through the divine will of God.

According to Vaisheshika, there exist many souls and they are liberated after repeated cycles of birth and death according to their karma by gaining knowledge. Understanding the atomic nature of the universe and the separation of matter and soul liberates a person. Liberation is complete absence of pain just as it is in Nyaya. In 11th century BC, Nyaya and Vaisheshika combined to form Nyaya-Vaisheshika Darshana.

Samkhya Darshana (Cosmic Principle School) was founded by Sage Kapila. It is based on dualism and postulates two eternal and ultimate realities, namely Purusha and Prakriti. The Purusha is consciousness, the Cosmic Spirit and Prakriti is Nature, the source of all material existence. While bondage belongs to Prakriti, Purusha is eternally free. Prakriti is inactive, unconscious, and in a state of balance of the three innate tendencies or Gunas. When Prakriti comes in contact with Purusha, its balance is disturbed and it becomes manifest, evolving 23 Tattvas or aspects of reality that constitute human experience.

The union of Purusha and Prakriti, gives birth to the Jiva or individual. Bound with Prakriti, Purusha gets confused and identifies itself with the physical body, which results in all forms of misery, suffering and pain. Liberation or Kaivalya is achieved when Purusha realises its true nature. Kaivalya includes absence of misery, presence of peace, and freedom from rebirth.

Samkhya describes the 23 Tattvas through which we experience the world. The five instruments of knowledge, the five senses are called Jnanendriyas and the five instruments of action are called Karmendriyas. The means with which the impressions are stored in human beings are the five Tanmatras. The external world is described through five Panchabhutas—space, air, fire, water and earth. The above are 20 tattvas. Buddhi (intellect), Ahankara (ego), and Manas (mind) are the other three tattvas. Together they help us to perceive and experience the external and internal universe. Samkhya is silent on God, neither refuting nor accepting its existence.

Yoga Darshana (Yoga School) is based on the Yoga Sutras written by Sage Patanjali in 3rd century BC. Yoga is derived from the root *yuj* which means 'to yoke', referring to the union of the individual soul with the Divine. Union with the Divine is not possible with an agitated mind, it has to be calmed first. The primary method of mind control is through concentration on any chosen object, which could be any part of the body, breath, mantra, idea or deity.

According to Yoga Darshana, mind is the storehouse of all conscious, subconscious and even unconscious impressions. These impressions give rise to thoughts, leading to action, creating further impressions and actions, and the cycle goes on. The constant fluctuations in the mind do not allow the Truth to be revealed. The stilling of the mind leads to revelation and hence liberation.

Yoga Darshana teaches the eight-fold path of controlling the body, mind, and intellect, which includes yama, niyama, asana, pranayama, pratyahara, dharana, dhyana and samadhi.

Yoga accepts Samkhya philosophy regarding separation of soul and matter, soul and thoughts and the concepts of ego, mind and intelligence. It accepts God as the Teacher of teachers, but not as a creator.

Purva or Karma Mimamsa (Ritualistic School) was founded by Sage Jaimini in 4th century BC. It is known as Purva Mimamsa since it deals with the earlier portions or the Karma Kanda or the rituals of the Veda. The text prescribes six means to gain knowledge. First is Perception through the five sense organs and the mind. Second is Inference based on observation and reasoning. Third is Comparison, by which conditional knowledge is derived. Fourth is Word or written knowledge from a reliable source. Fifth is Postulation based on circumstances. Sixth is Non-perception or knowledge based on non-existence.

The Darshana claims that physical universe and souls are real and permanent. The souls are many, and after death a soul enters a new body based on past karma. All cosmic manifestation is the result of karma or activities. It says that Veda are eternal and supreme and dharma means rituals and social duties. It justifies Vedic rituals and affirms that by respecting and observing them, one can achieve liberation.

According to this system, the source of knowledge of dharma is verbal cognition or the knowledge of words and their meanings. Dharma is following the commandments of the Veda and the other scriptures related to the Veda. It says that one who follows the teachings of the Veda and acts accordingly is sure to go to the heaven.

Uttara or Brahma Mimamsa (Vedanta School) deals with the concluding portions of the Veda, the Jnana Kanda or Vedanta, or the philosophy of the Upanishads. It was propounded by Sage Vyasa. The text focuses on understanding the nature of Reality and Self. It investigates the relationship between Brahman and the individual Self. It believes that Brahman is the highest reality and the master of all beings.

It explains the process of identifying Jeevatma, the individual soul with Brahman, the universal soul that is the Supreme Reality. It also offers a possibility of Jeevatma being both distinct and similar to Brahman.

Uttara Mimamsa believes that all diversity has been integrated into a unified whole. It highlights the study and interpretation of scriptures. It regards them as a means to attain self-realisation and liberation.

With the exception of the Yoga Sutras which offer a method of reaching the goal of life, and which are studied even today, Darshanas are philosophies and not revelations. Nyaya and Vaisheshika have indirectly influenced the practice of religion and spirituality, though Samkhya has been more influential. The Purva Mimamsa with its exclusive focus on the Vedic rituals has few followers. However, Vedic rituals are still practised and there are many religious schools which teach Vedic chanting, performance of rituals, and so on. Uttara Mimamsa or Vedanta is more popular, with lectures, talks and books being devoted to it.

12

VEDANTA SUTRA

Vedanta Sutra is considered as a supplement to Veda. It contains the essence of Vedic knowledge found in the Upanishads in a concise manner.

Sage Vyasa enquired into the Jnana Kanda of the Veda, the Aranyaka and Upanishad, and came to the conclusion that they represent the ultimate purpose of the Vedas. He compiled and distilled the absolute truth contained in the Vedas and explained it through logic and arguments.

Vedanta Sutra expounds that the Absolute Truth found in the Upanishad is the supreme reality of Godhead and he is the cause of everything in the universe. Hence it is also known as Brahma Sutra. It is one of three most sacred texts of Hinduism, the other two being the Upanishads and Bhagavad Gita.

Vedanta Sutra discusses the ultimate goal of life through logic and argument relating to cause and effect, and is therefore known as Nyaya Prasthana as well. Prasthana means origin or source. Since the Sutra deals with renunciation or sannyasa, it is also called Bhikshu Sutra.

The four chapters or adhyayas of Vedanta Sutra are Samanvaya, Avirodha, Sadhana and Phala.

Samanvaya Adhyaya has harmony as its central theme. It brings out the essential harmony in what all the seemingly diverse Upanishads say. The text establishes that Brahman is the Ultimate Reality. It is the origin of everything, it is the original cause of creation, sustenance and destruction of the universe.

Avirodha Adhyaya discusses and refutes the objections to Vedanta philosophy by certain schools of thought, who refuse to accept Brahman being the Primary Cause. The text proves that Brahman is both material as well as the basis of the world.

Sadhana Adhyaya deals with salvation. It says that knowledge of Brahman is the purpose of life. It explains how human birth is an opportunity to work out the karmas and attain liberation. It reiterates that knowledge, omniscience and bliss should be meditated upon, as they are the essence of Brahman.

Phala Adhyaya exhorts one to follow the methods of gaining knowledge of Brahman and then describes the result of that knowledge. It says that knowledge once gained should be shared with others. The benefits of knowing Brahman are described as bliss and the removal of the effects of karma.

There are interpretations or commentaries on the Vedanta Sutra, based on which, six systems of philosophy have emerged. Of these, Advaita, Dvaita, and Vishishtadvaita are more popular than Dvaitadvaita, Shuddhadvaita and Achintya Bhedabheda.

Advaita Vedanta is a non-dualistic school of philosophy founded by Adi Shankaracharya in the 8th century. It teaches that the Ultimate Reality, Brahman, is formless, infinite, and the only true existence. The individual Self, also known as Atman, is identical with Brahman, and the perception of duality or separation is an illusion or Maya. Liberation (moksha) is achieved only through realising this oneness by transcending the ego and ignorance. Advaita emphasises Self-inquiry and the knowledge of the Self as the path to spiritual liberation, where the distinction between the Self and the universe dissolves into unity.

Dvaita Vedanta is a dualistic school of philosophy founded by Madhvacharya in the 13th century. It posits a clear distinction between the individual soul (atman) and the Supreme Being, Vishnu or Brahman. In Dvaita, God is independent, while the soul and the material world are dependent on him. The philosophy rejects the idea that the soul is identical to Brahman, emphasising instead on an eternal difference between the two. Liberation (moksha) is attained through devotion (bhakti) and total surrender to Vishnu, recognising the soul's subservience and eternal difference from God, and seeking his grace for salvation.

Vishishtadvaita, a specific non-dualistic philosophy founded by Ramanujacharya in the 11th century, teaches that while Brahman (God) is one, it includes diversity within unity. Brahman is identified with Vishnu, who is both the material and efficient cause of the universe. The individual soul (atman) and the world are real but are distinct parts of Brahman, not identical with it. Souls retain their individuality even in liberation, yet they are inseparably connected to Brahman. Salvation (moksha) is achieved through loving devotion (bhakti) to Vishnu, surrendering to his will, and realising the soul's relationship with God as an eternal servant.

Dvaitadvaita, or duality in unity, is a school of philosophy attributed to Nimbarkacharya, combining elements of dualism and non-dualism. Founded in the 12th century, it teaches that the formless Brahman transforms itself into the world of duality, without losing its entity as the Absolute. The individual Jiva in his real nature is one with Brahman, but gets differentiated from it in the state of bondage by the adjuncts of body-mind. In liberation, the individual Jiva becomes one with Brahman like a river with the ocean. This philosophy does not preach devotion to any kind of deity.

Shuddhadvaita, or pure non-dualism, is a philosophical school founded by Vallabhacharya in the 16th century. It teaches that Brahman, identified with Krishna, is the Only Reality, and the world and souls are real, not illusions. Unlike other non-dualistic systems, Shuddhadvaita asserts that there is no distinction between Brahman and the world; everything is a manifestation of Krishna's divine play (leela). The soul is eternally connected to Krishna and retains individuality while being part of the divine. Liberation (moksha) is attained through grace and devotion (bhakti) to Krishna, recognising and participating in his divine essence and joy.

Achintya Bhedabheda, founded by Chaitanya Mahaprabhu in the 16th century, is a Vaishnava philosophy that harmonises dualism and non-dualism. It teaches that the individual soul (atman) and the supreme being, Krishna, are simultaneously distinct (Bheda) and non-distinct (Abheda). The relationship between the soul and Krishna is described as Achintya (inconceivable) because it transcends human logic. The world is real, and both difference and oneness coexist within Krishna. Devotional service (bhakti) to Krishna, characterised by love and surrender, is the path to liberation (moksha), where the soul realises its eternal, loving relationship with God while maintaining its individuality.

13

AGAMA

Agama means 'that which has come' and by implication, that which has been handed down from the past to the present. They are theological treatises and practical manuals relating to the worship of the Divine as Saguna Brahman (*saguna* means with attributes) and are the primary authority for any ritual or yajna. There is no clear consensus on when the Agama were written.

The Upanishad ask the spiritual aspirant to renounce all worldly joys, whereas the Agama accept the world as real and not as something to be renounced. They recognise that worshipping a personal God suits most people and prescribe proper rituals, symbols and mantras for such worship. Temples are built and worship is performed using the rules laid down in Agama texts.

Another major departure from the Vedic rituals is the use of idols and their worship in the Agama. Vedic rituals do not require idols or temples. They are based on invoking the formless devas (gods) usually through Agni (fire). The Agama also contain rules about the worship of other gods like Ganesha, Surya and Skanda. Even when seeking liberation, the Agama allow worship of God with form, unlike the Upanishad which do not mention any idol worship.

Though they may not derive their authority from them, they may differ even, but the Agama are not antagonistic to the Veda.

There are three major Agamas, the Vaishnava, Shaiva and Shakta, to suit the different mindsets of people. Some people view the world as real and God as immanent in the universe. For them, Vishnu is the immanent God that pervades everything. Then there are those for whom the world is no doubt real, but the Ultimate Reality is transcendent. Shiva is the transcendent God for them. For yet another lot of people, God is Power. For them, the Divine Mother is all powerful and is called Shakti, or power.

Although the three Agamas have different philosophies, all of them accept that there is a non-material soul that is essentially divine and that the purpose of life is its realisation. The inner aspects of the Agama practices link the individual, the mind and the senses to the divine. Externally, it has rituals, symbols, worship, idols and temples. Devotion is a central aspect in the practices.

The Shakta Agamas are referred to as Tantras, though the Agamic traditions as a whole may sometimes be called Tantrism.

Each Agama has four parts. The first one is Jnana Pada, dedicated to philosophical and spiritual knowledge. The second, Yoga Pada is related to the practices that lead to higher states of consciousness. The third, Kriya Pada lays down rules and regulations for esoteric rituals. The fourth, Charya Pada explains the conduct of religious rituals, sacrifices and festivals.

There are 108 Vaishnava Agamas, 28 Shaiva Agamas, 64 Shakta Agamas and numerous Upa Agamas.

Vaishnava Agamas serve as important texts in the Vaishnavism tradition, focusing on the worship of Vishnu and his various forms. They provide guidelines for temple construction, rituals, and the daily worship of deities. The Vaishnava Agamas are divided into four main categories:

Vaikhanasa, Pancharatra, Pratishthasara, and Vijnana Lalita, though they may sometimes be collectively addressed as Pancharatra. Each of these texts emphasises different aspects of devotion and ritual practices, offering a comprehensive guide to both the spiritual and practical aspects of worship. The Pancharatra Agamas, in particular, are highly influential, advocating the concept of bhakti (devotion) as the primary means of attaining liberation (moksha). The Vaishnava Agamas are central to the liturgical practices in many South Indian temples, influencing not just religious rituals but also temple architecture and iconography.

Shaiva Agamas are sacred scriptures in the Shaivism tradition, focusing on the worship of Lord Shiva. They are foundational to the rituals, temple construction, and philosophical teachings of Shaivism. The Shaiva Agamas are divided into four main categories: Karanagama, Charyagama, Kriyagama, and Yogagama, each addressing different aspects of spiritual practice, from rituals and worship to yogic practices and meditation. These texts emphasise the importance of both external worship (such as temple rituals) and internal worship (such as meditation and spiritual discipline). The Agamas also provide detailed guidelines for the construction and consecration of Shiva temples, as well as the creation of sacred icons and images. Central to the Agamas is the concept of creation, preservation, destruction, concealment, and grace—the five activities of Shiva governing the cosmic order. The Shaiva Agamas have given rise to two important schools of philosophy known as Shaiva Siddhanta prevalent in South India and Kashmiri Shaivism found in Kashmir.

Shakta Agamas, also known as Tantras, are sacred scriptures central to the Shaktism tradition, which venerates the Divine Feminine, primarily in the form of Goddess Shakti. These texts offer comprehensive teachings on rituals, worship practices, and esoteric knowledge aimed at spiritual empowerment and liberation (moksha). The Shakta Agamas are divided into three main categories—Kaula, Samaya, and Mishra, each reflecting different approaches to the worship of Shakti. These texts detail various rituals, including mantra chanting, yantra (sacred diagrams) creation, and specific ceremonies for invoking the Goddess' power. They also emphasise the importance of both external worship in temples and internal practices such as meditation and the awakening of the Kundalini energy. The Shakta Agamas provide a framework for understanding the universe as a manifestation of Shakti, who embodies both the dynamic energy and the nurturing, creative force of the cosmos.

14

KALA SHASTRA

Kalas are different sciences that are an important part of ancient Hindu scriptures.

Akshara Laksha Shastra is authored by Sage Valmiki and deals with 325 branches of mathematics including arithmetic, algebra, geometry, trigonometry, pure and applied mathematics. Consisting of about 50 chapters, the initial portion of the book explains mathematics and the latter deals with different energies that make up the world and keep it in motion. The text also deals with methods of measuring gaseous pressure, various aspects and effects of heat, light, static and current electricity, geology, geography, air, mineralogy, etc. It is believed that the earlier discoveries and writings of Sage Kashyapa, Sage Jaimini, Ganapati, Surya, Brihaspati, and Anjaneya formed the basis for this work.

Chitra Karma Shastra is the science of fine arts, consisting of a dozen chapters with more than 200 sketches. Written by Bhima, it teaches the method by which an artist can create the figure of a person after having seen only a small portion of their body, even if it's just a bone or a single hair.

Dhatuvada Shastra is a treatise on dhatu or primary substances of matter, their reactions, combinations, and transmutations, in other words, chemistry. It is written by Ashwini Kumars. The text also deals with the science of alchemy or the conversion of baser metals into gold.

Gaja Shastra deals with the behaviour and characteristics of elephants, and gives the methodology of how to categorise elephants on the basis of certain bodily marks. It discusses 16 methods of testing the various marks on the body of elephants. This science of elephants is written by Kumara Swami.

Kaala Nirnaya Shastra or the science of time was written by Lord Kartikeya. It deals with the concept of time, auspicious and inauspicious occasions, limitations of time and its measurements, and the presiding deities of various dates. It also analyses the division of time into moments, their classification into auspicious and inauspicious moments, and the deities presiding over each of those moments.

Lakshana Shastra is written by Sage Sakatayana. It is a science that deals with determination of sex in animate and inanimate creation. It also deals with the characteristics of a girl that can reveal her future, her family life, children, and prosperity.

Mahendra Jala Shastra is the science of magic, written by Veerabahu. The text describes the art of creating illusions like levitation, walking on water, and all such things that are included in the performance of magic shows.

Malinee Shastra is written by Sage Rishyashringa. Its 16 chapters deal with the science of flowers and their arrangements. It is the study of different styles of flower arrangements, how women should adorn themselves with flowers, construction of garlands and bouquets with varieties of flowers of different shapes and colours.

Malla Shastra, attributed to Malla Muni, is science of gymnastics and sports. Spread over three volumes, the work explains 82 kinds of athletic activities, their principles and methods, along with 24 kinds of infantry warfare where hand to hand combat is involved. It deals with wrestling, body-building, aerobics, games, exercises and other wide-ranging physical activities necessary for preservation of health.

Parakaya Pravesh Shastra is attributed to Sage Valakhilyas. It is the branch of science that deals with the knowledge of life entering into one body from another body. It analyses 32 kinds of yogas and 8 types of siddhis or superhuman capabilities. The text explains the ashta siddhis: anima, mahima, laghuma, garima, isitwa, vasitwa, prapti, and prakasya, leading to Parakaya Pravesh, which is the transference of one's soul at will to another body, as was done by Adi Shankara into the body of King Amaruka.

Ratna Pariksha Shastra is written by Vatsyayana. It is the science of testing precious stones and gold for their genuineness. The text deals with 24 characteristics of precious stones and gems, both natural and artificial. Their forms and weights are also discussed and classified. It describes 32 different ways of testing the quality and genuineness of precious stones.

Sakuna Shastra is written by Sage Garga. It is an elaborate treatise dealing with the good and bad effects of the sounds of birds and speech of humans. It says that when we set off towards a place, the person we meet coming from the opposite direction, or the sounds of birds and animals, provide indications of success or failure of our mission.

Samudrika Shastra deals with the various marks on the body which are said to indicate the type of person, their character, life and experiences. Palmistry is a branch of this science. It is believed that this shastra was first given by the Lord of the Ocean, Varuna, who noticed the auspicious marks on the body of Lord Vishnu reclining on Adishesha.

Saudamini Kala Shastra was written by Sage Matanga. It analyses the method of attracting anything through shadows and thoughts, and also seeing of the interiors of earth and the mountains.

Shabda Shastra is written by Sage Kandika. It is the branch of science which deals with sounds, echoes of moving and non-moving objects in creation, and their categorisation and modification. In its five chapters, the text also deals with capturing as well as mechanically reproducing sounds, and measurement of the pitch, frequency and velocity of sound.

Shakti Tantra Shastra is attributed to Sage Agastya. It has eight chapters. The text deals with Maya, Prakriti, the 64 kinds of external forces or energies in nature, the sun, moon and their powers (shakti), as well as the practical applications and harnessing of such forces. The unlimited energy contained in the atom, fusion, fission, and nuclear science, have also been well conceived in this work.

Shilpa Shastra is written by Sage Kashyapa. It is a science dealing with the construction of shrines, temples, castles, fortress, palaces, assembly halls, and so on. The text, in 22 chapters, describes 307 varieties of sculptures, 11 types of construction of places of worship, and more than 100 types of sacred images, their dimensions, proportions and other characteristics. Earlier works on this subject by Vishwakarma, Maya, Maruti, and Chhayapurasha, are integrated in Shilpa Sastra.

Supa Shastra deals with the science of cookery and is attributed to Sukesa. He has analysed 108 varieties of preparations and 3,032 kinds of dishes. Various kinds of preparations, pickles, condiments, sweets, puddings, etc., to suit the tastes of people in different parts of the world are described in details.

Turanga Shastra is the science of horses, written by Agnivarma. It's a treatise on everything about horses, their breeding, upbringing, pedigree, and points on how to select horses for various uses, including war. It analyses the different types of horses, their auspicious marks, their physiology, and training.

Vatavarana Shastra is the science of the clouds, attributed to Sage Atri, and deals with categorisation of clouds. The text explains 12 kinds of clouds, their characteristics, 12 kinds of rains, 64 kinds of lightning and 32 varieties of thunderbolts.

Visha Shastra is an exhaustive treatise on the science of poisons by Ashwini Kumaras. All poisons have been divided into 32 categories, and their properties, preparation, applications, effects and antidotes have been elaborately dealt with.

Yantra Shastra is written by Sage Bharadwaja. It is the science of vehicles. The text describes 339 different types of vehicles for movement on land, 783 kinds of vessels to be used on water for navigation, as well as 101 different varieties of airships. This text also deals with the possibility and methods of movement in space without the help of any vehicle, only by the application of mantras and cosmic diagrams or yantras.

15

OTHER IMPORTANT TEXTS

Anukramanika

The Anukramanika (also known as Anukramani) is a specialised text that serves as an index or catalogue for the Vedic hymns and mantras. Its primary function is to provide an organised and detailed reference to the structure and content of the Veda, particularly by listing each hymn, its author, the associated deity, the meter, and other contextual details. It offers clarity on the origin and purpose of the hymns, helping in the accurate recitation and preservation of the Vedic corpus. Each Vedic hymn has an associated Anukramani.

The most famous Anukramanika is Katyayana's Sarvanukramani, associated with the Rig Veda. This text is invaluable for Vedic scholars as it ensures that the sacred chants are recited with the correct intonation, context, and meaning, preserving the oral tradition that has been passed down for millennia.

The role of the Anukramanika extends beyond just cataloguing. It reflects the deep importance of precision in the Vedic tradition, as knowing the background of each hymn enhances its spiritual and ritualistic significance. These texts serve as essential tools for priests and scholars to maintain the integrity of the Veda.

Bhashya

A Bhashya is a detailed commentary on sacred Hindu texts, primarily the Veda, Upanishads, Bhagavad Gita, and Brahma Sutras. Unlike the original scriptures, which are often terse and symbolic, a Bhashya elaborates on their meanings, offering interpretations that make these texts accessible to scholars and practitioners alike.

Some of the most renowned Bhashyas were authored by great philosophers like Adi Shankaracharya, Ramanujacharya, and Madhvacharya, each interpreting texts through their own philosophical lenses—Advaita (non-dualism), Vishishtadvaita (qualified non-dualism), and Dvaita (dualism), respectively.

The purpose of a Bhashya is to clarify obscure or complex passages, resolve apparent contradictions, and provide a framework for understanding the deeper metaphysical and ethical teachings within Hinduism. These commentaries have played a crucial role in shaping the philosophical and theological discourse within Hinduism, ensuring the relevance of ancient scriptures for future generations.

Vrit (Vritti), Vartika and Tippani

Vrit or Vritti is a concise commentary that primarily aims to explain the basic meaning of a text, often serving as a guide for those new to studying complex scriptures. It simplifies dense philosophical ideas, making them accessible to a wider audience without heavy critical analysis. For example, in the context of the Yoga Sutras of Patanjali, many Vrittis are written to explain the aphorisms in simple terms. They don't add new philosophical insights but help with understanding the literal meaning.

A Vrit is typically brief, focusing on essential definitions, interpretations, and sometimes offering practical applications of the ideas. They are tremendously useful, mainly to students and beginners who need basic clarity on the text without the complexity of deeper analysis or multiple interpretations.

Vartika is more advanced than a Vrit. It not only explains but also expands, critiques, and analyses an existing commentary (like a Bhashya or Vrit). The writer of a Vartika is often an expert who engages critically with the original text and its commentary.

The purpose of a Vartika is to engage with the text on a deeper level, questioning, analysing, and sometimes refuting or refining the earlier commentary. It often addresses points that were omitted or insufficiently explored by the original commentator. For example, Kumarila Bhatta's Vartika on Jaimini's Mimamsa Sutras critically examines and expands the Bhashya written by Sabara Swamin. This Vartika addresses logical and philosophical aspects that require further explanation.

A Vartika isdetailed and often divided into sections that cover both the explanations of the primary text and philosophical discourse. It typically involves dialogue or discussion of various interpretations, and is useful to scholars, philosophers, and advanced students seeking a more profound, critical understanding of the text.

Tippani is the most focused and often the briefest of the three, providing explanations, clarifications of specific terms, phrases, or passages in a text or commentary.

It addresses particular issues, such as linguistic nuances, difficult terms, or obscure references within a text. The purpose is to enhance comprehension, focusing on the micro-level rather than offering broad explanations. A Tippani would explain archaic or complex Sanskrit terms used in the Bhagavad Gita or Upanishads, providing context or suggesting alternative translations.

It is typically in the form of marginal notes, interlinear comments, or short annotations attached to specific words or phrases. It doesn't provide a full analysis but focuses on specific difficulties in the text. A Tippani is meant primarily for students and scholars who already have a basic understanding of the text but need help with technical details or linguistic challenges.

If we compare the three, Vrit offers a surface-level explanation, whereas Vartika provides a critical, in-depth exploration and expands upon the text or commentary, and Tippani focuses on specific issues or terms, often technical or linguistic.

Vrit is for beginners or students, Vartika is aimed at scholars and advanced students, while Tippani is useful for those who already have a working knowledge of the text but need clarification on specific points.

Suppose there's a sacred text like the Brahma Sutras, a Vrit would provide a basic explanation of each aphorism, a Vartika might engage with an earlier commentator, like Shankaracharya's Bhashya, offering more profound insights or critiquing his interpretations, a Tippani might explain complex terms used in the Sutras or in the commentary, helping to clarify subtle linguistic issues.

These three forms of commentaries represent different layers of understanding of Hindu scriptures, helping the seekers delve according to their need and interest. They ensure that Hindu philosophical and spiritual wisdom is accessible for future generations.

In addition to the above, there are numerous scriptures in vernacular languages as well as translations from Sanskrit works. Covering all the Indian scriptures is beyond the scope of this book…in fact any one book.

REFERENCES

1. *The Principal Upanishads* by S. Radhakrishnan / Harper Collins
2. *The Sacred Books of the East,* Ed. Max Muller / Motilal Banarsidass
3. *Hindu Spirituality, Vedas through Vedanta,* Ed. Krishna Sivaraman / Motilal Banarsidass
4. *Hindu Scriptures,* Ed. Dominic Goodall / Motilal Banarsidass
5. *Outlines of Indian Philosophy* by M. Hiriyanna / Motilal Banarsidass
6. *The Wisdom of the Hindus,* Ed. Brian Brown / Garden City Publishing, USA
7. *The Three Branches of India's Life Tree* by Sri Chinmoy / Aum Publications, USA
8. *Sanatana Dharma: An Elementary Textbook of Hindu Religion and Ethics* / published by the Board of Trustees Central Hindu College Benares
9. *All about Hinduism* by Sri Swami Sivananda / Divine Life Society
10. *The Vedas* by Sri Chandrasekharendra Saraswati/Bharatiya Vidya Bhavan
11. *Brahma Sutras* by Swami Vireswarananda / Advaita Ashram
12. *The Upanishads* by Sri Aurobindo / Sri Aurobindo Ashram
13. *The Complete Works of Swami Vivekananda* / Vedanta-nl.org
14. *The Gospel of Sri Ramakrishna* / Ramakrishnavivekananda.info
15. *The Greatness of the Vedas* by Jeffrey Armstrong / Saibaba.ws

ABOUT THE AUTHOR

Sunita Pant Bansal is a renowned mythologist, storyteller, and author with a career that spans over four decades. Throughout her journey, she has worn many hats, excelling as a writer, editor, publisher, and entrepreneur.

She has headed publishing houses and founded and edited newspapers and magazines for readers in India, US and UK. Her contributions to the world of literature extend across multiple platforms, working with prestigious organizations such as Walt Disney, Warner Bros., Pearson Education, *The Times of India*, *Hindustan Times*, and ABP Group.

In addition to her global collaborations, Sunita ran her own publishing house creating books for audiences worldwide and served as the President of the esteemed Institute of Indology, further cementing her influence in the literary world.

Sunita has authored over 30 books for adults and young readers, delving into the philosophy of mythology. She has also written innumerable children's books focused on folk literature and scriptures, which have been translated into multiple languages and sold across the globe. Her books explore and reinterpret the timeless tales of characters from the epics and foundational texts for modern readers. Her storytelling blends mythology with history, making ancient tales accessible in today's context.

Sunita's contributions to publishing and literature have earned her recognition, including the 2024 AALEKH Women Achievers Award.

Amongst Sunita's recent bestsellers are *The Return of Vikram and Betaal, Everyday Gita, Puranas: The Origin of Gods and Goddesses, Ramayan: The Journey of Ram, Mahabharat: The Rise and Fall of Heroes.*

Website: www.sunitapantbansal.com
LinkedIn & Instagram: @sunitapantbansal
Twitter & Facebook: @sunitapb

Readomania

Readomania exists to nurture, curate, and bring to you content you love. We are a publishing house that takes pride in encouraging talent, new or old, and provide a wonderful platform for awesome stories.

We make this possible in multiple ways.

The first as an independent publishing house. Readomania boasts of multiple imprints across various categories—fiction, nonfiction, children, to name a few. An eclectic mix of content for its readers, when you read a Readomania title, you enter a world that's yours, supported by unique and quality narratives.

The second, as an online publishing platform for writers—a place to share stories, poems, opinions, travelogues, a way to explore your creative talent. Available as premium, as well as free-to-read content across multiple genres, the reader is spoilt for choice.

Join us in this journey, as we explore, develop, and present stories to our readers and audiences. Welcome to the world of Readomania, get ready to craft stories that enrich lives.

You can visit us at: www.readomania.com